Doers
of the
Word

Putting Your Faith
into Practice

DOERS
OF THE
WORD

PUTTING YOUR FAITH
INTO PRACTICE

ARCHBISHOP TIMOTHY M. DOLAN

Our Sunday Visitor Publishing Division
Our Sunday Visitor, Inc.
Huntington, Indiana 46750

CONTENTS

PREFACE

*D*uring my seven happy years as Archbishop of Milwaukee, I spent a chunk of each day in my cozy chapel in the basement of my house.

The home where I lived was secluded and tranquil, in the acreage of Saint Francis de Sales Seminary, which, while only ten minutes from our Cathedral downtown, was still a pristine forest on the shores of Lake Michigan. So, my cherished moments of prayer in my basement chapel were serene, calm, quiet, undistracted.

When I arrived in New York as archbishop, I found my residence to be smack dab in the heart of bustling mid-town Manhattan. My chapel in this historic home is attractive indeed ... but hardly cloistered or noiseless! Now, as I pray, I hear cars and horns, jackhammers and sirens, laughter and curses, crowds and parades.

At first, I admit, I pined for the recluse of my Lake Michigan "cave"! But now, I have come to savor the clamor of my new chapel just as much.

And I've come to conclude that both settings are conducive to meditation and reflection.

Yes, at times I need the coziness and peace of my basement chapel in the woods, where the only noise was the turning of the pages of my Bible. But I also need to meet the Lord in the midst of His created world, with all the clutter, cacophony, and craziness of Madison and 50th.

He's there in the stillness; He's there in the messiness.

Most of the essays contained in this book were comprised in one of those two chapels. What is so clear is that we have a Lord who is present in the silence of the human heart, as He was in the desert and on the mountaintop, and in the babel and clamor of Bethlehem and Calvary.

He's there ... our call is to serve Him, discover Him, and find Him.

That's all these reflections are — my clumsy yet sincere response to His constant invitation to discern His presence and His direction in all the ups and downs of life.

Thanks for trusting that I might be of some little help to you in responding to the same promptings from our good and generous God.

Thanks, Gwen, Barb, and Del for your help; thanks, Our Sunday Visitor, especially Bert Ghezzi and Woodeene Koenig-Bricker, for your assistance.

Thanks, most of all, dear Lord, who's there on both Lake Michigan and Madison Avenue!

✠ Timothy M. Dolan
Archbishop of New York
September 14, 2009
Feast of the Triumph of the Cross
Year for Priests

CHAPTER ONE

My Lord and My God

A New Beginning

For God, every day is New Year's.

Every day the sun rises is His act of confidence that creation continues.

Every baby born is His act of hope that humanity goes on.

Every marriage is His trust that love is stronger than hate.

Every morning brings a new chance.

Every prayer a new hope.

Every blocked path a new route.

Every sin repented a fresh burst of grace.

Every mistake a lesson learned.

Every death a new life.

We have a God who relishes fresh starts, new dreams, trying again, resolutions made.

He is the Lord of second chances.

He never tires of giving us another opportunity.

❧

Turn again, O God of hosts;
  look down from heaven, and see;
have regard for this vine,
the stock that your right hand planted.
They have burned it with fire, they have cut it down;
  may they perish at the rebuke of your countenance.
But let your hand be upon the one at your right hand,
  the one whom you made strong for yourself.
Then we will never turn back from you;
  give us life, and we will call on your name.
Restore us, O LORD God of hosts;
  let your face shine, that we may be saved.

— PSALM 80:14–19

What the World Needs

Thomas Paine said, "These are the times that try men's souls." It's just as true today as it was at the time when our country was founded.

In this time of want, we center on what — check that, whom — we really need: a Savior. In these years of war, terrorism, and violence, we long for the Prince of Peace.

In this period of economic stress, we renew our hope in the only One who never fails us.

In this time when we are scared, we listen again to the angels who told Mary, Joseph, and the shepherds, "Be not afraid."

In this period when the "culture of death" looms and threatens, we exalt that the Son of God was a baby in the womb.

In a culture that believes all truth and morality to be relative, that religion is a farce, and that one is only enlightened when liberated from faith , we join the truly wise men in kneeling before the newborn savior of the world.

When miracles seem absurd and noble love impossible, we contemplate that Holy Night when a virgin gave birth, a star dispelled darkness, a manger became a throne, a stable a palace, when sheep and cattle provided warmth and straw a bed, and lowly shepherds found the way, the truth, and the life.

When emptiness of soul or cynicism of heart leaves us inwardly hungry, we behold a baby born in a little town called "house of bread," in a manger where food for the livestock was stored, and receive the "Bread of Life" in the Eucharist.

When the world is turned upside down, a virgin gives birth, winter is spring, night is day, a star is the sun, the silent night is filled with angelic song, and the harsh coldness of life is filled with the warmth and tenderness that can only come from the One who never changes: Jesus Christ, "the same, yesterday, today, and tomorrow."

❦

The name Bethlehem comes from the old Hebrew meaning "house of bread." Micah 5:2 is often cited as a prophetical text referring to the birthplace of the Messiah:

> *But you, O Bethlehem of Ephrathah,*
>   *who are one of the little clans of Judah,*
> *from you shall come forth for me*
>   *one who is to rule in Israel,*
> *whose origin is from of old, from ancient days.*

But did you know that Scripture actually refers to two Bethlehems? Bethlehem of Zebulon was a small town north of Nazareth that is mentioned in Joshua 19:15. Bethlehem of Judea, located about six miles south of Jerusalem, is the city we know as the birthplace of both King David and Jesus.

The Gift of the Ordinary

On Christmas, we see Jesus being born. On the Feast of the Epiphany, we behold Him as a baby in the crib worshipped by the Wise Men. The next Sunday, the Feast of the Baptism of the Lord, we see Him thirty years old.

Where did the time go?

How did He grow up so fast?

What did He do for thirty years?

We don't really know, do we? All we know is that He lived at Nazareth and grew up under Mary and Joseph. His life was plain, simple, routine.

We call it the "hidden life." And that in and of itself is profound.

In spending 90 percent of his earthly life unseen and unrecorded, He teaches us:

- The value of silence. Except for his cryptic remark to Mary when she found Him in the temple when He was twelve, "Did you not know I must be in my Father's house" (Lk 2:49), He speaks not a word.
- The significance of family life, as He grows up in a home, loved and formed by faithful parents.
- The gift of work, as He was known as "the carpenter's son" (Mt 13:55).
- The necessity of preparation, as He spent three decades getting ready for His three years of public ministry.
- The value of religion, as He was raised a faithful, devout, observant, practicing Jew.

Do you think your life tedious, fatiguing, boring, desperate, uneventful, humdrum, and monotonous?

You are in good company... the company of the One who spent thirty years of hidden life at Nazareth.

❧

Although we call Joseph a carpenter, he was actually a "tekton," an accomplished craftsman. His skills would have been a cross between a designer, an architect, and a construction engineer, not a simple furniture or cabinet maker. Working alongside Joseph, Jesus would have become an artisan in wood, stone, and even metal. Some modern archaeologists speculate that with their expertise, Jesus and Joseph may even have worked on the massive construction projects commissioned by Herod the Great in Caesarea, which included a deep-sea harbor, baths, and numerous public buildings.

The Sign of the Cross

In many ways, the cross is our sign of identity, a mark that we belong to Christ.

During a visit to a prison in southeastern Wisconsin, an inmate explained to me the meaning of the various tattoos I could not miss on the arms of some of the prisoners. Each gang, he explained, has its own tattoo, its own "brand," as it were. There is no mistaking to whom the convict belongs. His gang claims him, has dominion over him, protects him, and watches out for him. All the other inmates recognize to whom he belongs, because of the sign, the brand, the tattoo.

Well, we are convicts, too. We have been convicted of sin, and been sentenced to death.

But our sentence has been commuted, we have been redeemed, we have been declared innocent and free, and our debt has been paid, by the precious blood of the Son of God.

We belong to his "gang," the Church. He has claimed us. He has dominion over us. We now belong to Him. We, too, have a sign, a brand, so there's no mistaking to whom we belong: the sign of the Cross.

We trace this Cross on ourselves, especially before prayer and worship. It hangs around our necks. It hangs in our homes, offices, classrooms, meeting rooms, hospital rooms. It is the way we identify ourselves as belonging to the Lord.

By God's mercy, at the gates of heaven, we will not be asked for an ID, a passport, a driver's license, or a stock portfolio, but the gatekeeper will look for the sign of the Cross.

Is it visible in your life?

❧

The sign of the Cross is one of the most ancient symbols of Christianity. As early as the end of the second century A.D., the Church Father Tertullian writes, "In all our travels and movements in all our coming in and going out, in putting on our shoes, at the bath, at the table, in lighting our candles, in lying down, in sitting down, whatever employment occupieth us, we mark our foreheads with the sign of the Cross."

True God and True Man

It is so clear from the stirring gospel account of Jesus raising His friend Lazarus from the dead that Jesus is a true man. His humanity is so evident. As Pope Benedict often remarks, "We have a God with a human face." Yes, our God, Jesus Christ, had good friends, Martha, Mary, and Lazarus among them. He enjoyed their company and hospitality at their little home in Bethany; and He was overcome with emotion and sadness when Lazarus died.

Jesus Christ is true man.

His divinity is also clearly evident in this passage. He can raise the dead. He is Lord of the living and the dead. He is the "resurrection and the life."

Jesus Christ is true God.

This God-man is in the business of transformation, renewal, change. He does this a lot. He changes water into wine, sin into grace, bondage into freedom, hate into love, sickness into health, doubt into faith, despair into hope.

He brings us from death to new life by transforming Good Friday into Easter Sunday.

Let us pray the words of the Divine Praises:

Blessed be God.
Blessed be his Holy Name.
Blessed be Jesus Christ, true God and true man!

❧

The Divine Praises are a series of acclamations originally written in Italian in 1797 by Luigi Felici, S.J., to make reparation for profanity or blasphemy. They were expanded by Pope Pius VII in 1801 and now include praise of the Immaculate Conception, the Assumption, the Sacred Heart, St. Joseph, and the Precious Blood. They are usually said after Benediction, but they can be prayed anytime.

A Fool for Christ

The wonderful Irish Sisters of Mercy who taught me at Holy Infant Grade School in Ballwin, Missouri, cautioned us about taking April Fools' Day too seriously. It was, they said, a commemoration of the day the soldiers tortured and made fun of Jesus as a clown, a fool, a loser, a reject.

The April 1 theory of the sisters wasn't historically correct, but they were right to remind us that Our Lord was mocked as a fool. The elite, the powerful, the rulers, the "movers and shakers," the cultured class, the intellectuals, dismissed Him as a failure, a joke, someone to make fun of.

Guess what? His followers nearly 2,000 years later can at times be treated the same way.

People who believe in Jesus as the way, the truth, and the life, who take His Church and His teaching seriously, can expect to be ridiculed by some media, family, neighbors, coworkers, comedians, or talk show hosts.

Those who put faith in values, convictions, or realities that cannot be scientifically validated are dismissed as crackpots, irrational, opposed to progress and reason.

His disciples of today, who hold that His love is forever and that He invites us to share it for all eternity, are sneered at as using religion as a crutch to get through life's challenges, as "pie-in-the-sky," to avoid life's demands.

People who admit that their most cherished convictions — often flowing from their faith — have a bearing on their political decisions are mocked as dangerous theocrats.

His followers of today who believe that our worth comes in *who we are* not *what we have*; that life is an inviolable gift to be protected, not an inconvenience to be extinguished; that sexual love is so sacred we save it for marriage; that love, forgiveness, and reconciliation trump hate, revenge, and conflict, can all expect to be treated as fools.

Yes, Jesus was called a fool, and those who dare follow Him can expect the same.

And not just on April 1.

❧

In Medieval Europe, most people celebrated New Year's for a week, starting on March 25, the Feast of the Annunciation, and ending on April 1. In 1582, Pope Gregory XIII introduced the Gregorian calendar that replaced the old Julian calendar, which had become out of synch with the solar calendar by 10 days. The new calendar set January 1 as New Year's Day. Because news traveled slowly in those days, many people either didn't learn about the change or refused to accept it and continued to celebrate New Year's on April 1. They were called "fools" and were subject to practical jokes and ridicule. Even after the "new" calendar was widely adopted, April 1 continued to be a day of mirth and pranks.

High Holy Days

For our Jewish neighbors, the "high holy days" are the blessed moments between Rosh Hashanah and Yom Kippur, when they come together as families, as congregations, to pray and celebrate. For our Islamic neighbors, the great season of Ramadan plays a similar role.

During their special days, both of these great religions stress renewal, conversion of heart, reconciliation with God and others, repentance, and recommitment during these sacred times.

Those themes are integral to us Christians as well, aren't they? We also have seasons — Advent, Christmas, Lent, Easter — when we concentrate on these same noble messages. This leads me to conclude that the world religions have a lot more that unites us than divides us.

As Pope Benedict XVI often preaches, true religion unites, not divides; forgives, not broods; helps, not hurts; loves, not hates. The true faithful are not radicals but reconcilers. Another characteristic that unites the great world religions is the act of trusting a loving, providential God in times of turmoil and trouble.

We cannot allow the fanatics to kidnap the true spirit of belief and religion.

Every religion tragically has them. We see persecution of Christians today in the Middle East region, India, and parts of Africa. Jews have been and are viciously hounded, and we Christians hardly have a perfect record on the way we have treated Jews, Muslims, and other believers throughout our long history.

It's time to claim that those who preach hate, urge violence, and hold that "religion" justifies oppression, coercion, and attacks on others are the real infidels and heretics, and definitely do not represent authentic religious faith.

Renewal, reconciliation, repentance, trust in God — Jews, Catholics, and Muslims are united in holding such values high, in never flagging in their pursuit, and in encouraging each other in seeking them!

❧

Rosh Hashanah marks the start of the Jewish New Year. Celebrated on the first and second days of the seventh month of the Jewish calendar, it generally occurs in early fall. Yom Kippur, also called the Day of Atonement, is observed on the tenth day and is the most sacred of the Jewish holidays. It is a day set aside to seek forgiveness for the sins of the past year, as well the final day of the ten days of repentance (Days of Awe) that begin with Rosh Hashanah (see Leviticus 23:23–27).

Ramadan is the ninth month of the Islamic calendar, a time of fasting and prayer during which devout Muslims do not eat or drink from sunrise to sunset. Muhammad is believed to have received the Qur'an during one of the nights of Ramadan.

Trust in Divine Providence

I am only half joking when I tell you that one of my favorite quotes from the Bible comes from Psalm 127: "God gives to his beloved in sleep" (v. 2, NAB). It's true that I enjoy a good night's sleep — and even a siesta on my day off — but it's also true that God's blessings can come to us as we "sleep on it."

To wait, to take a little time in making a decision, to "see how it looks in the morning," guards against rashness, impatience, and impetuosity.

Slumber is an act of trust in divine providence. We realize we've done our best and must surrender control. We let go, confident God will watch over us.

I get dozens of e-mails a day. Some of them are mean and petty. My inclination is to fire a sharp retort back. That makes me as uncharitable as the sender. So, I've developed a strategy. I never reply until I've "slept on it." Same with a tough letter or pointed telephone call. If I reply rashly, I usually regret it later. Better to wait until morning.

This has saved me from a lot of sins against patience and love.

It is true: "God gives to his beloved in sleep." In the morning, I discover a new angle, a fresh insight, a calmer, more prudent approach.

I urge you to trust in God's care and allow him to give you wisdom and understanding — all while you are getting a good night's sleep.

❧

"I should be distressed that I drop off to sleep during my prayers and during my thanksgiving after Holy Communion. But I don't feel at all distressed. I know that children are just as dear to their parents whether they are asleep or awake, and I know that doctors put their patients to sleep before they operate. So I just think that God knows our frame; he remembers that we are dust."

— ST. THÉRÈSE OF LISIEUX

CHAPTER TWO

Signs of Faith

The Sacraments

The word "sacrament" comes from the Latin *sacramentum*, which means "a sign of the sacred." The old Baltimore catechism defined sacraments as "outward signs instituted by Christ to give grace." Some snicker a bit now at the old definition, and I'll admit there are better ones. But I also wonder if we have lost our trust in the power of the sacraments to give grace.

The gospel teaches us about grace when Jesus says, "We [Father, Son, and Holy Spirit] will come to them and make our home with them" (Jn 14:23). That's good news, isn't it, that God dwells in the heart and soul of the believers?

The intensification of that divine life comes to us dramatically, personally, and powerfully in each of the sacraments. Baptism, Eucharist, Confirmation, Reconciliation, Anointing of the Sick, Matrimony, and Holy Orders are not acts we perform to show God our worthiness, to earn His gifts, to merit His love. They are gifts of grace He gives us.

Those seven sacraments are humble moments when we simply and with childlike trust admit that we very much need the Lord's life, love, mercy, and strength. They're not about us doing God a favor, but asking Him to do us a favor.

It will come as no surprise that the Latin word for favor is *gratia* — grace!

Recently, I visited a dying woman in the hospital. When I called to ask her if I could come visit her in hospice, she paused. "Archbishop, I really appreciate your calls to me and my family. And I'll be thrilled to see you here for a visit. All of that is a big help. But," she paused again, "if you really want to help me, when you come, please hear my confession, anoint me, and bring me Holy Communion. That will be the best help of all."

She understood the grace and power of the Sacraments.

May we all do likewise.

✿

Sacraments are "powers that comes forth" from the Body of Christ (cf. Lk 5:17; 6:19; 8:46), which is ever-living and life-giving. They are actions of the Holy Spirit at work in his Body, the Church. They are "the masterworks of God" in the new and everlasting covenant.

— CCC 1116

Union with Jesus

Recently, I had an engaging conversation with a man who had recently entered our Catholic faith. That in itself is hardly extraordinary. What was unique about this gentleman was that he had been an ordained minister in his former church. I asked him, "What most attracted you to our Catholic faith?"

"The Sacraments!" he answered immediately, "I want the grace and mercy, the intimate union with Jesus Christ, that I believe powerfully comes to us in the seven Sacraments of the Church!"

He went on to explain that his former faith — which he still loves and respects — had what he termed a "soft" sacramental system: Baptism, occasional Eucharist, and Confirmation. But he told me that these were not considered at the heart of the Church. His own extensive study of the Bible, the early Church, the Fathers of the Church — those legendary teachers and preachers of the first centuries of the Church whose towering intellects, theological depth, and personal sanctity make them normative in Catholic doctrine — and the early Ecumenical Councils of the Church, had led him to the conclusion that the Church was all about Sacraments. He quoted St. Leo the Great, "All the power and reality of our Holy Redeemer [Jesus] are now visible in the Sacraments of the Church."

I was hardly surprised by his reply. While they might not use the same vocabulary as this man, new converts often tell me the same thing: they want, they are eager for the Sacraments of the Church. They believe the timeless teaching of our Catholic faith that the seven Sacraments are indeed gifts from Christ to continue — personally, powerfully, really, and truly — His saving presence, His lavish grace, mercy, healing, and salvation here on earth are unfailing ways to bring us to Jesus.

Each sacrament has an outward, material sign that is an essential part. For instance, baptism must be performed with water. The Eucharist must be celebrated with grape wine and wheat bread. The Sacrament of the Sick must be administered with the use of holy oil. In some cases, like Reconciliation, the sign is the words spoken by the priest, but in all cases, the sacraments have certain concrete actions associated with them to help us understand when the grace of the sacrament is applied.

The Lord's Day

When Jesus rose from the dead, not only did reality change, not only did our lives change, not only did our relationship with God change, but even the calendar changed.

As His birth changed the way we number the years, so His rising from the dead altered the way we plan the week.

The resurrection was of such earthquake proportions that his followers felt compelled to gather on that day each week and profess their faith in the reality of His saving death and Resurrection.

It's the same today, 2,000 years later. An essential part of our Catholic faith is that we gather for the Eucharist every Sunday. It is our Sabbath. In Latin languages, it is called "The Lord's Day," *Dominica* in Italian and *Domingo* in Spanish. The English name — Sunday — comes from the Latin *dies solis*, meaning "the sun's day," but surely we can think of it as "The Son's Day" as well.

Jesus, the Son, told us, "Strive first for the kingdom of God" (Mt 6:33). That means making God the priority in our lives. A very telling way we followers of Christ do that is by literally giving Him the first day of every week.

Now, I know I'm preaching to the choir here, as most of you already take Sunday very seriously, and have Sunday Mass as a non-negotiable in your spiritual lives. But we all know someone who may need to be reminded that every Sunday is Easter. I exhort us all to reclaim Sundays, the very day of His resurrection, as our Sabbath, as His day, as The Son's Day, when we are faithful to the tradition which is as old as the Church herself — the celebration of the Eucharist.

❧

The word "Sabbath" comes from the Hebrew word "Shabbat," which means "to cease." The order to keep the Sabbath holy by refraining from undue labor is the third of the Ten Commandments. For Jews of Jesus' time, the Sabbath began at sundown on Friday and ended at sundown on Saturday. In keeping with the biblical way of reckoning, the Saturday vigil thus counts as Sunday Mass for Catholics. Jews still maintain Saturday as their holy day and Muslims observe Fridays.

The Sacred Liturgy

I wonder if I did the right thing," she asked me after Mass. A mother of a teenage daughter, she went on to explain her dilemma.

"My daughter was asked over to some friends to watch a movie on the passion and death of Christ. The friends are not Catholic, but they are wonderfully believing Christians. They had invited a group over to read the gospel story of the passion, watch the movie, and then have common prayer and discussion."

"I was thrilled to let my daughter go," the mom went on, "until she told me this would take the place of her Sunday Mass. If she went to that, she reasoned, she would not need to go to Mass."

"Well, what did you decide?" I asked the mother.

"I told my daughter that the movie and the group would be all about how the passion happened, while the Sunday Liturgy was about the passion happening. So a movie could never take the place of Mass."

Mom was right: the Liturgy is not just about what happened way back then; it's about what is happening now. The paschal mystery — the suffering, death, and resurrection of Jesus — is renewed at every sacred liturgy. Yes, we remember, but we also relive.

The Mass is not, then, a movie or a "passion play," but the actual renewal of those pivotal redemptive moments, for we believe that the dying and rising of Jesus is of infinite, eternal value, and that we are absorbed into it every time we come together for the Sacred Liturgy.

This is especially clear during Holy Week. On Palm Sunday, as the opening invitation bids us, we accompany Christ right now, with lively devotion and faith, as He enters Jerusalem. On Holy Thursday, the Last Supper is renewed, not just recalled, as we are at the table with the Master the evening before He died. On Good Friday, we are "there as they crucify my Lord," not just in a nostalgic way, but reliving it again in the Liturgy of the Lord's Passion. On Holy Saturday, at the Easter Vigil, we behold the Resurrection, as Christ conquers sin, Satan, and death now in the Easter sacraments of Baptism, Confirmation, and Eucharist.

The Liturgy is not just a compelling story of earth-shaking events that happened long ago. It is where these saving events continue, are renewed, and happen in the here and now for us today!

✺

A Passion Play is the dramatic reenactment of the last hours of Jesus' life from his trial to his death on the Cross. It is probably derived from the reading of the Gospel reading of Good Friday, when various celebrants would sing the different parts. The earliest true Passion Plays developed in Germany during the 1300s, reached their zenith in the 1500s, and generally fell out of favor after the Protestant Reformation. The Oberammergau Passion Play, which has been performed since 1634 by the inhabitants of the village of Oberammergau in Bavaria, is the most notable exception.

The Importance of Silence

Do you think we need more silence at Mass? Experts weigh in on that question.

The first set of such experts is you, God's People, especially those faithful to Sunday Mass. I often hear how you very much appreciate a warm, friendly, welcoming atmosphere at Church. People greet one another before and after Mass, and there are even whispered greetings in Church itself. That is good, you tell me. After all, the parish church is our spiritual home.

But then you also report to me that you miss the spirit of awesome, reverent silence that used to reign in our Churches. You worry that Sunday Mass has become just a social occasion, and that the Eucharist itself is cluttered with too much noise, music, announcements, and talking. As one of you remarked, "I talk to my neighbors all week. On Sunday I need to talk to God."

So the first response is mixed: warmth, friendliness, welcome — yes; too much chatter and noise — no.

Now, the second expert, Cardinal Godfried Danneels of Belgium, who actually helped write the revolutionary decree of the Second Vatican Council on the Liturgy, offers his opinion. At a lecture at Boston College, he worried that "the liturgy has become an unstoppable succession of words." Going on, he expressed concerns that the sacred rite has been "turned into a social event or a piece of theatre." When that happens, the cardinal concluded, we have tragically damaged the celebration of the Eucharist, because the center is no longer Christ, but ourselves.

He could be on to something: chatting, announcements, and "turn and greet your neighbors" before Mass; music, song, movement, words — nonstop — during Mass; applause, greetings, announcements.... Our liturgies have often become an "unstoppable succession of words."

Finally, expert number three. In his message on the Eucharist, *Sacramentum Caritatis*, Pope Benedict XVI both praises and urges full participation at Mass, but also encourages more silence before, during, and after the Eucharist. Christ is the central person at the Eucharist, and we need to create a space in our hearts for Him to pray with, in, and through us. Silence is one very effective way to do that. That's the suggestion of the Holy Father.

It sure is worth thinking about ... and now I'm going to be silent.

❦

"In life today, often noisy and dispersive, it is more important than ever to recover the capacity for inner silence and recollection. Eucharistic adoration permits this not only centered on the 'I' but more so in the company of that 'You' full of love who is Jesus Christ, 'the God who is near to us.'"
— BENEDICT XVI, SUNDAY, JUNE 10, 2007

Welcome Back

"Father, I'm afraid I'm a hypocrite," he said from his seat next to me on the airplane.

"Well," I replied, "if you are, nice to meet you, because so am I a lot of times. Now, tell me why you think you're a hypocrite."

It was late Sunday night. The plane back to Milwaukee was late, as flights seem always to be these days. I was tired, yet happy for his company, and the priest in me was eager to hear his story.

"Today was my little boy's First Communion," he began. "I was there. But, see, I'm afraid I'm not much of a dad to him. His mom and I split up four years ago. I don't see him as often as I should, especially now that I'm out of town. And boy, I've really been a flop Church-wise. Thank God his mom is good at praying with him, sending him to Catholic school, and taking him to Mass every Sunday. I'm an awful example. But this morning," he continued, choking up a bit, "I felt almost holy. There he was all dressed up, white coat and tie, hands folded, a little nervous. He looked like an angel. His mom and I actually smiled at each other as we watched him walk by. For just those few moments, all seemed right with God. I felt close to the Lord, grateful for my son, praying for him and his mom, and even kind of apologizing to God for being such a jerk. I wouldn't dare go to Communion, which hurt, but I sure believed, and wished I could've. I gave my boy an extra strong hug after Mass."

We talked a while longer. I told him that I didn't think he was a hypocrite at all, that Jesus would be happy with his honesty and sense of regret, and that the Lord was always ready to welcome him back.

I hope he returned. After all, it's never too late for a second chance with God. As Blessed Columba Marmion tells us, at every sacrament, we're again a baby in the arms of his or her parent at the baptismal font — pure, innocent, full of promise and hope.

❧

Blessed Columba Marmion (1858–1923) was an Irish priest who eventually joined the Benedictine Abbey of Maredsous in Belgium. He founded an abbey in Louvain where he served as a professor at the university there. A well-known retreat master and spiritual director, he was beatified on September 3, 2000, by Pope John Paul II.

A Different Vocation Crisis

June is still the most popular month for couples to get married, followed by August and May, but weddings can happen almost anytime these days. That is, when they do happen.

To put it bluntly, fewer and fewer people are getting married at all. Researchers tell us that only 50 percent of Americans are getting married — Catholics included.

Clearly, we have a vocation crisis in the sacrament of matrimony! When we pray for "an increase in vocations," we mean priests, sisters, and brothers, but we had better start adding, "For an increase in vocations to lifelong, life-giving marriage."

What's behind this dropoff in marriages? A lot of reasons are suggested by the experts: a fear of commitment; apprehension about marriage because this generation has seen so many fail; a preference for career and care for self rather than the selfless sacrifice marriage necessitates; and the convenience of "living together," which gives couples all the bonus without any of the onus of marriage.

I don't know what, if any, of those reasons lies at the root of the problem. But we have a problem. A lack of vocations to matrimony is a disaster for our country, for our Church, for humanity.

Recently, a very thoughtful, faithful Catholic observed to me that she believed a lifelong, life-giving, faithful marriage was no longer possible. "The Church is 'out of it' to expect that," she commented. "A successful, happy, permanent marriage is now no longer humanly possible."

All I could reply to her was, "I guess that's why it's a sacrament, because then we're assured of God's supernatural grace, which is stronger than any earthly problem."

"For an increase in vocations to lifelong, life-giving, faithful marriage, we pray to the Lord!"

"Lord, hear our prayer!"

∾⚬∾

Holy Father, to reveal the plan of your love, you made the union of husband and wife an image of the covenant between you and your people.

In the fulfillment of this sacrament, the marriage of Christian man and woman is a sign of the marriage between Christ and the Church.

Father, stretch out your hand, and bless all who are married.

— FROM THE NUPTIAL BLESSING AT A CATHOLIC WEDDING

Of Human Life

ope John Paul II often pointed out that we human beings are at our best when we give ourselves away in love to another. This happens dramatically in marriage, when a man and woman pledge themselves to each other unreservedly, for all time, committed to making their married love faithful, forever, loving, and life-giving. When a husband and wife express their selfless love most passionately in the very marital act, they give themselves to one another without holding anything back. This love is an act of trust in each other, and in God. That's what sex is all about. And, when the baby comes, their love literally is personified; it has a name.

On July 25, 1968, Pope Paul VI issued his encyclical letter *Humanae Vitae* (Of Human Life). As many of you recall, "all hell broke loose."

All most people can recall is that Pope Paul said no to artificial, chemical birth control. How oppressive! How insensitive! How authoritarian! How "out of it!" The dissent was vast and nonstop.

A reflective reading of the teaching shows, of course, that the Holy Father said *yes* to love, to life, and to the *Law of the Gift*. All he really taught was that the intimacy between a man and woman in marriage was love at its best, as a couple gave themselves to each other unreservedly, completely, holding nothing back, eager to see that their love was procreative, as they had the privilege of cooperating with the Lord in the creation of new life, a baby.

All the Pope was doing was reaffirming the Church's timeless wisdom, mined from nature and reason, that to block the procreative aspect of sexual love was to risk robbing it of its selfless, generous, trusting, sharing character, reducing it to an act of selfish pleasure only, no longer a divine act bringing about new life.

All Paul VI did was call us back to the divine intention that links love and new life. He worried that if we viewed sex only as a momentary thrill, not as an act flowing from faithful, lifelong, life-giving love, we and our world would be in big trouble.

❧

Responsible parenthood ... concerns the objective moral order which was established by God, and of which a right conscience is the true interpreter. In a word, the exercise of responsible parenthood requires that husband and wife, keeping a right order of priorities, recognize their own duties toward God, themselves, their families, and human society. From this it follows that they are not free to act as they choose in the service of transmitting life, as if it were wholly up to them to decide what is the right course to follow. On the contrary, they are bound to ensure that what they do corresponds to the will of God the Creator. The very nature of marriage and its use makes His will clear, while the constant teaching of the Church spells it out.

— *Humanae Vitae* II, 10[*]

When Did I See You?

Our savior, Our Lord, Our God was considered a criminal. The founder of our religion, who also happens to be the only-begotten Son of God, was arrested, tortured, jailed, convicted, and executed. His early followers hardly fared much better. The apos-

[*] http://www.vatican.va/holy_father/paul_vi/encyclicals/documents/hf_p-vi_enc_25071968_humanae-vitae_en.html

tles were often hauled into court, interrogated, arrested, tortured, and imprisoned.

It should not shock us, then, that those who follow Jesus have a special solicitude for prisoners.

I find my visits to our jails and time spent with inmates some of the most rewarding and fruitful in my apostolate. And I always leave those visits with a heightened sense of gratitude for our many priests, deacons, women and men religious, committed faithful, and devoted organizations who will be able to look the Master in the eye on judgment day and smile when he observes, "I was in prison, and you visited me" (Mt 25:36).

On one of my visits to a prison, the gospel had the risen Jesus "showing his wounds" (see Lk 24:39; Jn 20:20) to his disciples. I suggested that our Lord wants us to "show our wounds" to Him, and that a great place to do that is in our prayer, especially at the Eucharist.

I asked those in attendance if they had any wounds. Their nods, eyes, and whispered "yeses" said it all.

Wounds of regret? More nods.

Wounds of addiction? More glistening eyes.

Wounds of anger? More yeses.

Wounds of separation from spouses, children, families, friends? A crescendo of agreement.

Wounds from worry and discouragement about the future? Unanimous affirmation.

It was no homiletic prop to suggest to those there that day that they had a particular solidarity with the five mortal wounds of Jesus on the cross. It was no exaggeration to tell them that they should feel especially home at Mass, as Jesus shows us His wounds and invites us to show Him ours. And it is no surprise that I should feel called to spend more time with those in prison who teach me to share my own wounds.

✎

The corporal works of mercy are seven specific actions that both teach us compassion and help alleviate the suffering of others. They are:

- *Feed the hungry*
- *Give drink to the thirsty*
- *Clothe the naked*
- *Shelter the homeless*
- *Visit the sick*
- *Visit those in prison*
- *Bury the dead*

Matthew 25:31–46 lists the first six. The seventh probably comes from Joseph of Arimathea's burial of Jesus, as well as mention in the book of Tobit.

Christ and His Church

"Christ, yes! Church, no!"

This seems to be the chant these days. It seems many want a King without a kingdom, a shepherd but not a sheepfold, a general with no army, a spiritual family where I am the only child; faith but no faithful.

Believe, yes. Belong, no.

In short, they want Christ without his Church.

A recently published report on religion in America verifies this. A quarter of our people raised Catholic no longer consider themselves such. Some seem more loyal to the baseball team they cheered for as a kid than to the Church in which they were baptized and raised.

This, of course, is a sharp pastoral challenge to the Church. It cuts to the core of Catholicism, for, of course, we believe that Christ and His Church are one.

Jesus Christ and His Church are a package deal for a Catholic.

Think about it: when our Lord ascended into heaven, forty days after He rose from the dead, His disciples could well have split up and gone their separate ways as individuals. They could have said, "Why stick around? He's gone. I believe in Him. I'll go off on my own and try to live as he taught."

The first disciples would have none of that. "Stick together" was at the heart of His message. They believed in Him as a community, as a spiritual family. He was the vine; they were the branches. They were intimately united to Him and to each other. In company with His mother, they remained as one and prayed hard for the promised Holy Spirit. On Pentecost Sunday their prayers were answered.

So, from the very beginning, the Church was essential. Common prayer, unity in faith, mutual love and charity, Sunday Eucharist, rebirth into something beyond themselves by Baptism, strengthened in confirmation, sent out to invite others — these were the communal actions of the Church because the Church was Christ alive!

In other words, we are saved as part of His Church. This understanding of the unity between Christ and the Church moves us to rejoice in the Church as a golden bond keeping us tethered to Christ, not as handcuffs that we try to get unlocked.

As the Gospel says: He is the vine and we are the branches (see Jn 15:5)!

༄༅

When Pope Benedict XVI visited the United States in 2008, he spoke of the gift all have in the Church. "In a society which values personal freedom and autonomy, it is easy to lose sight of our dependence on others as well as the responsibilities that we bear towards them. This emphasis on individualism has even affected the church, giving rise to a form of piety which sometimes emphasizes our private relationship with God at the expense of our calling to be members of a redeemed community. Yet, from the beginning, God saw that 'it is not good that the man should be alone' (Gen 2:18). We were created as social beings who find fulfillment only in love for God and for our neighbor. If we are truly to gaze upon Him who is the source of our joy, we need to do it as members of the people of God. If this seems countercultural, this is simply further evidence of the urgent need for a new, renewed evangelization of culture."

CHAPTER THREE

In the Year of Our Lord

Advent

The reason I relish Advent so much is that, when you really think about it, life is an Advent.

We are always waiting, longing for, yearning for the meaning, purpose, light, mercy, and salvation that only God can give.

We look at our world and see violence, immorality, crime, war, abortion, poverty, starvation, injustice, suffering; we peer into ourselves and see sin, selfishness, darkness, emptiness. We turn to the Church and see scandal, problems, worries.

We're always in Advent. We need a messiah. We need someone to rescue us. We crave a savior.

Yet, in another way, the rescue operation has in fact occurred, the savior has come, "the long reign of sin has ended, a broken world has been renewed, and we are once again made whole."

We wait for him, but he's already here.

We need saving, yet we already have been saved.

Thus the tension between Advent and Christmas.

So we find ourselves, as I did the other evening, walking the corridor at St. Joseph's hospital, at the one end laughing with radiant young parents and their hour-old baby, and at the other end of the hall crying with parents in the neonatal intensive care unit.

Advent and Christmas

Darkness vs. light

Death against life

A pregnant woman understands all this. She feels both promise and cramps; she senses subtle hope, but has to wait so long. She will bring forth life through intense agony. She knows comfort and deliverance are on the way, but realizes they cannot be rushed.

The pregnant woman groans in agony; so does creation; so does the Church; so do we.

The pregnant woman sings to her God, "My soul magnifies the Lord... for the Mighty One has done great things for me" (Lk 1:47, 49).

And then, finally, the mother instructs, as she points to the "fruit of her womb," Jesus, "Do whatever he tells you" (Jn 2:5)!

❧

The word "Advent" derives from the Latin word adventus, meaning "coming," which itself is a translation of the Greek word parousia, which means "arrival." Because the word was often used in accord with official visits by royalty, it has come to be associated with Christ's Second Coming. Thus the season of Advent is both a time of waiting for Christmas and also a reminder that we wait for His return in triumph.

Angels Unaware

It was 4:30 a.m., a blustery December morning in D.C. I had been there the day before for meetings, and my flight home scheduled for the night before had been cancelled due to ice and snow. I was on stand-by for the first flight out Wednesday morning, if I could get to the airport before 5 a.m.

My mood was hardly the best.

I hailed a cab.

I was tired, cold, coughing. The driver had the radio on. We listened to news of shootings of kids on a school bus, bombings, and assassinations in the Middle East, war in various places around the world.

Christmas seemed far away, long ago.

The cabbie observed how dangerous the world was. After the news, he told me he and his family had fled a war-torn nation as refugees.

I commented how his job — driving a cab in the middle of the night in a city hardly known for its safety — was far from safe.

He turned on the light and pointed to the sun visor above him. There was an image of the Madonna and Child. (Mind you, he had no way of knowing I was a priest, as I had my scarf wrapped around my neck, covering my clerical collar.) "Jesus and Mary are my only protection," he informed me. "Yes, danger is everywhere. We can only be truly safe with them."

Some angel — a messenger from heaven — usually crosses my path every year as Christmas nears. When I entered Reagan National Airport, "Silent Night" was on the speaker. This year's angel came in the guise of a cabbie.

I'm glad I left him a good tip.

❧

"There is joy in the presence of the angels of God." (Lk 15:10)

"Do not neglect to show hospitality to strangers, for by doing that some have entertained angels without knowing it." (Heb 13:2)

"The soul at its highest is found like God, but an angel gives a closer idea of him. That is all an angel is: an idea of God." (Meister Eckhart)

"All God's angels come to us disguised." (James Russell Lowell)

Christmas

"That little baby is God," the big brother (he looked about six) explained to his little sister (she looked about four) on Christmas Eve, as they looked at the manger after Mass.

He, of course, was absolutely correct.

God loves us, and invites us to love Him back. He really wants us just to let Him love us — personally, passionately, forever.

How best to teach us that?

By becoming a baby!

We all want to pick a baby up, to snuggle the baby, to kiss him, hold her, rock him, and cuddle her. There is nothing more inviting, innocent, vulnerable than a baby.

Just think — God wants us to hold Him, love Him, cuddle Him, rock Him. That's how tender and accessible He is.

In the end, it's all about love, isn't it?

No one wrote more eloquently about God's love for us than John. He was our Lord's best friend. There he was, next to Him at the last supper, at the foot of the cross, caring for His mother. This Christmas season, spend some time reading the beautiful Gospel of John and seeing again, for the first time, just how much God loves each of us.

❧

Our familiar Nativity scene with Mary and Joseph, the Wise Men, the donkey, the ox, the sheep, and the shepherds was first presented by St. Francis of Assisi. During the 1223 Christmas season, he created a "living Nativity" with the hopes of inspiring renewed love and devotion to the Christ child. Today, Nativity scenes can be found all over the world. The Vatican has displayed a manger scene by a Christmas tree in St. Peter's Square since 1982.

Ordinary Time

*Y*esterday, as I set the Missal for the celebration of Mass, I saw those chilling words, "Monday of the First Week in Ordinary Time." Ugh!

For nearly two months, we've had "biggies" — Christ the King, Thanksgiving, Advent, Immaculate Conception, Our Lady of Guadalupe, Christmas, New Year, Epiphany, the Baptism of the Lord — and now it's *Ordinary Time.*

Yet, is not ordinary time — the day-in-day-out, humdrum treadmill, from hitting the snooze button on the alarm until we brush our teeth before bed — is this not what living our faith is all about?

It seems like we have a God who really liked ordinary time.

A God who prefers whispers to yelling, breezes to storms, those struggling through life to those who got it made.

A Lord who arrived as a baby, not a superman; who grew up obedient to a mother and father, not a child prodigy.

A Christ who chose a humble mother, not an elite socialite mother; twelve bumbling first followers, not slick résumé-holding interns.

A God who remains with us still in bread and wine, tears and smiles, family and friends, neighbors and community, awkward prayers, a beat-up book called the Bible, and the embrace and example of people who believe in him.

If He were here with us today (and, of course, He is), He'd be on the bus or driving in the lane next to us, punching a time card or at the desk in the adjoining office, making beds and washing dishes, doing homework and kneeling in prayer, staying up with the sick child or at the assisted living place with grandma, working the fields or manning the assembly line. In all times and in all ways, He would be trusting in His Father's love and eager to do His will.

Ours is truly a God of Ordinary Time.

༄

If you go to Mass on the Feast of the Baptism of the Lord, which is celebrated on the Sunday after Epiphany, you may be startled to see the next Sunday is "The Second Sunday of Ordinary Time." What happened to the First Sunday? It's a little confusing. The Sunday Masses for the Baptism of the Lord are the very last celebrations of the Christmas season. However, Evening Prayer that night is the first liturgical marker for Ordinary Time. Therefore, the first part of that Sunday is Christmas and the second part is Ordinary Time. The next day, Monday, is the "First Monday of Ordinary Time." Therefore, the next Sunday has to be "The Second Sunday in Ordinary Time," because it is the Sunday of the second week in Ordinary Time.

Holidays or Holy Days?

A daily newspaper here ran an article about February, calling it the "fun month." They pointed out Groundhog Day, February 2; Valentines Day, February 14; and Mardi Gras, which often falls in February. The article elaborated on food, drink, and partying possibilities for each of these days during "fun month."

It's interesting that we live in a secular culture, a society that ignores God and faith, or, at best, puts up with religion as long as it's private and attempts no public influence, and yet, all three of these "February fun events" are religious, sacred, and faith-based.

Groundhog Day is the Feast of the Presentation of the Lord, forty days after Christmas, when Jesus is proclaimed as the "light of the world." Thus we bless candles for liturgical use throughout the year, and sometimes refer to the feast as Candlemas Day. It finds meaning in the tug-of-war going on in nature between light and darkness. Which will win? Night or day? Darkness or light? Winter or Spring? It's the same question we ask when the groundhog looks for his shadow. And our faith tells us the answer: the sun, the light of the world, the Son, triumphs.

February 14, the Feast of St. Valentine, offers plenty of legends to choose from. Perhaps this priest in third century Rome had an apostolate of introducing Christian girls to Christian boys; or maybe he paid ransom to help free young women trapped in prostitution; or perhaps he encouraged the exchange of greetings expressing intentions of pure and chaste love between couples; or possibly his love for Jesus and His Church was so passionate that people claimed they could see his heart. No one knows for sure, but his feast day gives rise to one of the most popular occasions for expressions of love. Once again, a secular holiday is based on a religious feast!

And, finally, Mardi Gras, the final day before Lent, those forty days of more intense prayer, penance, and charity in preparation for the great feast of Easter. It's the "last party" before we begin a season of sacrifice and mortification. No Lent, no Mardi Gras.

I'm not so naïve as to believe that the popularity of these three "February fun days" shows a conversion from our secularism. Most people are totally unaware that Groundhog Day, Valentine's Day, or Mardi Gras are all rooted in a culture of faith and religion. But maybe we can at least smile at the fact that, while religious feasts might sadly fade, the yearnings that gave rise to them — the hope that light defeats darkness (Candlemas Day), that love enchants and endures (Valentine's Day), and that one prepares in anticipation of spiritual struggle (Mardi Gras) — are an innate and constitutive part of the human condition.

☙❧

The name Mardi Gras, French for Fat Tuesday, may have arisen because the French used to drive a fat ox through the streets of Paris on this day. Or it may refer to the fact it is the day before the strict fast of Lent begins and all the "fat" foods like meat, eggs, cheese, and butter had to be consumed before they went to waste. The latter is the reason it's sometimes called Pancake Tuesday — making pancakes out of all those eggs and milk was a good way to use them up. It's also called Shrove Tuesday because to shrive means to confess and it was common to confess one's sins before the start of Lent.

Time-out for Lent

"You're taking a 'time-out,'" Mary Theresa, my sister-in-law, says firmly through clinched teeth to her two daughters, Grace and Kathleen, my two angelic, innocent little nieces.

What it means, of course, is that they have been misbehaving, fighting, arguing, whatever, and the referee — Mom or Dad — calls for a time-out. It means the offending party has to go to her room, sit by herself, be quiet, settle down, think about what she was doing, resolve to behave, and then, come on out and join the rest of us.

At least in the case of Grace and Kathleen, time-outs seem to work. Within twenty minutes or so, they are back with us, usually more peaceful, contrite, and cooperative.

By now you know where I'm going with this. We have to admit we've been unruly, disruptive, and tough to get along with at times, demanding, impatient, selfish, not playing too well with the other kids, and not sharing our toys.

So, Holy Mother Church firmly declares an annual time-out — Lent!

Time is one of our most priceless possessions. We never seem to have enough of it. And we are reluctant to give it away or share it with others. Child psychologists tell us today's kids crave the time of their parents, just to be there with them. Marriage counselors observe that a happy marriage is impossible unless the couple spends quality time together.

The same is true of our relationship with the Lord. It takes time. If we do not give God time, our friendship with Him will be shallow and brittle.

Thus, we give God time the first day of the week, Sunday, as we worship Him at Mass;

Thus, we give the Lord time each morning and night with some prayer;

Thus, if we can, we strive to give Him quiet moments daily over Scripture, before the Blessed Sacrament, in a chair with our eyes closed — wherever, whenever, however....

But during Lent, we are called to sacrifice even more time for Him. Nothing in life is more worthwhile than our relationship with the Lord. Give it the time it requires.

Just listen to your mother — Holy Mother Church — as she proclaims, "It's Lent, and you need a time-out!"

❧

Have you ever wondered why we call the forty days before Easter "Lent?" In the Romance languages, the name of the season is based on the Latin quadragesima, *a translation from the Greek* tessarakoste *which literally means the "forti-eth day," referring to the forty days between Ash Wednesday and Easter. The word "Lent" comes from the Anglo Saxon* lencten *and simply means "Spring." In the Middle Ages, when sermons started being given in the vernacular, the Teutonic word for the season was adopted in place of the Latin.*

Via Dolorosa

Sometimes we call them by their Latin title, the *via crucis* ("way of the cross"), or the *via dolorosa* ("the sorrowful way"). More often we refer to them simply as the Stations of the Cross.

I love this devotion, and the Church especially encourages it during Lent. That's logical: Lent is the season of the year when we unite ourselves more closely to Christ in His suffering and death, and the Stations are one of the more tried and true methods of doing that.

As we say the Stations, we recite the words: "We adore Thee, O Christ, and we praise Thee! Because by Thy Holy Cross Thou hast redeemed the world."

This prayer goes back to St. Francis of Assisi. One of his passions in life was to make the love and mercy of God in Christ as real, as tangible, as accessible as possible. Just as he gave us the first crib for Christmas, he was responsible for encouraging this devotion as well.

The Stations are very simple. All we do is walk — really or mentally – fourteen stops on the road to Calvary from Jesus' unjust condemnation by the Roman governor, Pontius Pilate, to his burial in Joseph of Arimathea's tomb. The movement — physical or mental — reminds us that we, too, are called to an intimate share in the passion, death, and resurrection of Jesus, the paschal mystery. We meditate on Scripture at each site, pray, and enter into the reality of our Lord's suffering and death.

Some people have their favorite form of the Stations. St. Alphonsus, Cardinal Newman, and Fulton Sheen have all written meditations that are still used today. Other people enjoy their own thoughts, words, and prayers at each of the fourteen stops.

Some look forward to praying the Stations of the Cross communally during Lent, as we walk them along the walls of our churches; others prefer to make them privately, maybe from their own home, or at an outdoor shrine.

But, as St. Francis hoped, no matter how we pray the Stations, let us allow ourselves to be moved by the depth of God's love and mercy for us.

❧

In 1991, Pope John Paul II introduced the Scriptural Way of the Cross. In 2007, Pope Benedict XVI approved them for general use. All of these stations are based on the Gospel accounts of Jesus' Passion, whereas only eight of the traditional stations have clear Scriptural origins. The new stations are:

1. *Jesus in the Garden of Gethsemane*
2. *Jesus is betrayed by Judas and arrested*
3. *Jesus is condemned by the Sanhedrin*
4. *Jesus is denied by Peter*

5. *Jesus is judged by Pilate*

6. *Jesus is scourged and crowned with thorns*

7. *Jesus takes up His cross*

8. *Jesus is helped by Simon to carry His cross*

9. *Jesus meets the women of Jerusalem*

10. *Jesus is crucified*

11. *Jesus promises His kingdom to the repentant thief*

12. *Jesus entrusts Mary and John to each other*

13. *Jesus dies on the cross*

14. *Jesus is laid in the tomb*

Holy Week Passeggiata

During the happy years I spent in Italy, I grew fond of the Italian custom of a *passeggiata* — a casual stroll, always with a friend, usually after a good meal, in the evening when the sun began to set and the breezes arrived.

A *passeggiata* is a ritual. If someone asks you to go on a *passeggiata*, it is a compliment. It means he or she enjoys your company and wants to get to know you better. The conversation on this walk is usually substantive. You end it by having shared something significant with each other.

Holy Week is a *passeggiata*. Jesus invites us to take a walk with Him, to accompany Him on the way to His death and Resurrection. He wants us near, He wants us close, because He has important matters to confide in us.

We began on Palm Sunday, walking with Him on His entry into Jerusalem, waving palms and acclaiming Him our Lord, our Messiah, our Savior;

We'll take a *passeggiata* with Him Holy Thursday, after the Mass of the Lord's Supper, as we process with the Holy Eucharist to the altar of repose.

On Good Friday we walk with Him again, on the Way of the Cross, and process at the Liturgy of the Lord's Passion up to the cross to venerate it with a kiss.

On Holy Saturday, at the Easter Vigil, we process with the paschal candle from the new fire into the darkened church, proclaiming Christ as the light of the world. Then we take a *passeggiata* with those to be baptized back to the font.

Holy Week is a week of walking, accompanying, knowing.

Hopefully, when we are finished with this annual *passeggiata*, we're much better friends with Jesus.

The Pilgrimage of Etheria, an account of a woman who visited the Holy Land around 381–384, contains the first detailed account of the way Holy Week was observed in the early church. About Good Friday, she writes: "And when they arrive before the Cross, the daylight is already growing bright. There, the passage from the Gospel is read where the Lord is brought before Pilate, with everything that is written concerning that which Pilate spoke to the Lord or to the Jews.... And afterwards the bishop... addresses them thus: 'Go now, each one of you, to your houses, and sit down awhile, and all of you be ready here just before the second hour of the day, that from that hour to the sixth you may be able to behold the holy wood of the Cross... then from the sixth hour we must all assemble again in this place, that is, before the Cross, that we may apply ourselves to readings and to prayers until night.'"

Everything Depends on Easter

*J*ust yesterday, it seems, I was eating *paczki,* those delicious, plump, sweet, round rolls, covered with sugar with a tasty filling in the middle that the Polish use to celebrate on Mardi Gras. I thoroughly enjoyed a few *paczkis*, dunked into a mug of hot chocolate, with whipped cream on top, after a good *carnivale* ("farewell, meat!") meal because, as St. Paul says in 1 Corinthians 5:6–8, "Clean out the old yeast so that you may be a new batch.... For our paschal lamb, Christ, has been sacrificed. Therefore, let us celebrate the festival, not with the old yeast, the yeast of malice and evil, but with the unleavened bread of sincerity and truth."

Fresh yeast.

New life.

Easter.

Everything in life depends on Easter, doesn't it? Whether or not you believe in Easter, when Jesus "passed over" from death to life, is the most pivotal decision one can make.

The answer to that question — do you believe in Easter? — resolves most of the other nagging questions in life: in the end, what will win?

Death or life?

Despair or hope?

Hate or love?

Darkness or light?

Winter or spring?

Doubt or faith?

Nothingness or eternity?

Getting or giving?

Bullies or nice guys?

Hell or heaven?

Revenge or mercy?

Snow or sun?
Tears or laughter?
Isolation or unity?
Tension or tenderness?

It really all depends on Easter, doesn't it?

❧

Calculating the date of Easter isn't easy. In general, Easter is the first Sunday after the first full moon after the vernal equinox. To be completely precise, Easter falls on the first Sunday following the ecclesiastical full moon (which isn't quite the same as the astronomical Full Moon) that occurs on or after the day of the vernal equinox which is fixed as March 21. Oh, and the ecclesiastical full moon is the fourteenth day of a new moon. Essentially all this means that Easter can never occur before March 22 or later than April 25. To determine the date for any given year, it's best just to look it up.

The Spirit of Pentecost

As a boy, I idolized John F. Kennedy. I will never forget catching a glimpse of him on Sutton Avenue in Maplewood, Missouri, as he passed by in the backseat of a convertible. That he was of Irish decent, and a Catholic, only added to his heroic status in my ten-year-old mind. One of the saddest days in my life remains November 22, 1963. Even though subsequent historical scholarship has more soberly assessed the limits of his person and his presidency, I must confess he still remains high in my pantheon of heroes.

I remember well when the eternal flame was ignited at his grave in Arlington Cemetery. It seemed so appropriate: this great leader's "spirit" would remain alive. His ideals, his dreams, his goals, would never be extinguished. His "spirit" would always be with us, never to burn out.

At Pentecost we remember the Spirit of another man, only this man also happens to be the one true God. His Spirit is not just a vivid memory, not only inspirational ideas, not just an eternal flame, but a Person, the third Person of the Most Blessed Trinity, God the Holy Spirit.

The Holy Spirit is the most overlooked and taken-for-granted Person of the Trinity. No wonder. The Spirit's actions and power — without which we would not have life itself, either human or divine — are subtle, gentle, hushed, internal, soft, and invisible. Let us never take for granted this Divine Person whose presence and power is so essential, so effective, so ubiquitous, so much a part of our lives.

❦

A "sequence" is a chant or hymn that is sung or recited during the Liturgy of the Word prior to the reading of the Gospel. Veni Creator Spiritus (Come, Creator Spirit), the Pentecost Sequence, is believed to have been written by a German monk, Rabanus Maurus, in the ninth century:

> *O Holy Spirit by whose breath*
> *Life rises vibrant out of death:*
> *Come to create, renew, inspire;*
> *Come, kindle in our hearts your fire.*
>
> *You are the seeker's sure resource,*
> *Of burning love, the living source,*
> *Protector in the midst of strife,*
> *The giver and the Lord of life....*

In you God's energy is shown,
To us your varied gifts made known.
Teach us to speak, teach us to hear;
Yours is the tongue and yours the ear.

Flood our dull senses with your light;
In mutual love our hearts unite.
Your power the whole creation fills;
Confirm our weak, uncertain wills.

From inner strife grant us release;
Turn nations to the ways of peace.
To fuller life your people bring
That as one body we may sing:

Praise to the Father, Christ his Word,
And to the Spirit, God the Lord:
To them all honor, glory be
Both now and in eternity. Amen.*

The Sacred Heart of Jesus

$\mathcal{I}$ have always found the image of the Sacred Heart of Jesus to be consoling. To think that "my Lord and my God," Jesus, has a heart literally on fire with love for me gives me a lot of strength and hope.

Apparently it gives our Holy Father hope too. Speaking extemporaneously at the Coliseum after leading the Way of the Cross on Good Friday evening 2007, Pope Benedict XVI remarked: "Our God is not a remote God, intangible in his blessedness. Our God has

---

* *Veni, Creator Spiritus,* attributed to Rabanus Maurus (776–856). Adapted from *Liturgy of the Hours,* trans. Anon. (New York: Catholic Book Publishing Company, 1976), II, 1011.

a heart. Indeed, he has a heart of flesh; he was made flesh precisely to be able to suffer with us and to be with us in our suffering."

I don't know about you, but I find the Holy Father's words downright moving.

I'm glad we have a Lord whose heart can break, be wounded with thorns, and burn with passionate love and mercy for us. That's one reason that each morning I pray as I was taught in second grade:

> All for Thee, Most Sacred Heart of Jesus!
> Sacred Heart of Jesus, I place all my trust in Thee!
> Sacred Heart of Jesus, I believe in your love for me!
> Sacred Heart of Jesus, have mercy on me a sinner!
> Sacred Heart of Jesus, Thy kingdom come!

∼❧∼

Love for the Sacred Heart of Jesus has a long tradition in the Church, but the devotion as we know it was promulgated by St. Margaret Mary Alacoque in the seventeenth century. In a series of revelations, Jesus revealed twelve promises to her, including blessing every place where a picture of the Sacred Heart is displayed and that all who receive Communion on the First Friday of nine consecutive months will not die without receiving the sacraments.

The Dance of Nature

Autumn. I bask in the crisp air, royal blue skies, bracing breezes, and symphony of colors. It's as if nature is resisting the onslaught of winter, wanting to preserve the life and growth of spring and summer. Nature will lose this battle, but will win the war, because spring will again triumph.

Autumn also preaches about the providence of a loving God who tenderly orders the precision of the universe. The dance of nature moving gingerly from summer to winter is so hypnotic that we want the Divine Choreographer to come out for a curtain call!

Our lives are seasonal, too, aren't they? Because fall is a transitional time, it can serve as a reflection of the movements in our lives:

> Birth and death
> Work and unemployment
> Health to sickness
> Love to loneliness
> Grace or sin
> Hope or despair
> Settled-in or "on the move"
> Prosperity or recession
> Peace or war

Yet fall highlights the paradox of our lives as well. Like us, nature is always in flux, but we also know there is an anchor that gives nature and the seasons an order and predictability. So, while autumn tells us that nature is in transition, it also hints at the eternal law at the core of reality.

So it is with our lives. There are times that shattering change occurs in our lives. But, at the deepest level of reality and meaning, we discover a firm foundation, an "unmoved mover," an immutable base resting on a loving, caring, omniscient, omnipotent, providential God.

Fall showcases a tree that is transfigured before our eyes, but remains a tree. Yet, like that work of art, a tree in autumn, life maintains a constant identity, a reliable rooting, in the Lord, and in Jesus Christ, "the same yesterday, today, and tomorrow."

❧

Cardinal John Henry Newman, observed, "In the next life it will not be so, but here, to live is to change, and to live long is to change often." Cardinal Newman, a convert from the Anglican Church, was a major thinker, writer, and theologian of the late nineteenth century. Catholic chaplaincies on university and college campuses — Newman Centers — are named after him. He was named "Venerable" in 1991.

Pray For Us

Do you pray for the dead?

Not only is it a wonderful act of charity, recommended in the Bible (see 2 Macabees 23:45–46), but it is also good for us.

We usually pray for the faithful departed with one or more purposes in mind.

One, we want to praise God for the life of someone who has had a loving impact on us. The lives of parents, grandparents, spouses, friends were gifts to us from God, and we naturally and laudably want to thank Him for the life of the deceased with our grateful prayers.

Two, while we of course can never "earn" a deceased person's salvation — eternal life is a completely unmerited gift to us from God, our Father, achieved only by the dying and rising of Jesus — we can ask the Lord's mercy on the souls of our beloved faithful departed. We Catholics have a long tradition of praying for the souls in purgatory, confident that God's powerful mercy hardly ends at death.

Three, our reverent and grateful prayer for the dead is a tangible way of showing our membership in the Communion of Saints. Our beloved deceased are not dead but alive, now, we trust and hope, with God for all eternity. They're still part of the spiritual family we call the Church, part of this Communion of Saints. Where they have gone, we hope one day to be, and a big part of heaven's joy will be our reunion with them.

Four, we pray for those mourning the departed. That's why we go to wakes and funerals: to be in prayerful solidarity with our friends who are grieving. We want to support them, and the best way to do that is by praying with and for them.

Finally, we pray for ourselves. The death of someone close to us is always a "wake-up call." It reminds us of our own fragility, our own mortality. It nudges us to our final goal: heaven.

"Eternal rest grant to them, O Lord! And let perpetual light shine on them. May they rest in peace! Amen!"

***

All Souls' Day is one of the more recent additions to the Church calendar, if you consider that it was accepted in Rome only in the fourteenth century. But remembering the dead in prayer dates back to the time of the earliest martyrs, as attested to by inscriptions on the walls of the catacombs. In 998, St. Odilo of Cluny formally established the custom of praying for holy souls on November 2 at his monastery. From there the practice spread throughout France and eventually to the entire Church.

CHAPTER FOUR

We Are the Branches

Ever Ancient, Ever New

Every time I'm in Rome, I pass a church made famous by St. Philip Neri, who is buried inside it. Its cornerstone was laid in 1599, but it's called the *Chiesa Nuova*, which means the "new church." Imagine, Rome's "new" church is nearly 200 years older than the Archdiocese of Baltimore, the oldest diocese in the United States!

Despite the fact that the Church has a long and enduring history, we in the United States are still young. We were, after all, considered a "missionary church" until 1908. When I went to Rome as rector of the North American College in 1994, I offered to teach a course at the Gregorian University on the history of the Catholic Church in the United States. One of my colleagues, a church historian, teased me, "But that could be done in just a couple of lectures. You're still just babies!"

Youth has its advantages: We are growing, we are vibrant, we wonder and ask questions, we are trying to make our way and find our place, we are dreaming and hoping.

And it has disadvantages: We bristle and get impatient, we question timeless wisdom and tradition, and we are tempted to think we know better, that our elders should listen to us more than we need be attentive to them. We can at times be saucy and brash.

The Church needs both youth and age. She is, after all, the Body of Christ. At times, that Body of Christ is like the bouncing baby at Bethlehem, filled with life, hope, promise, the future. At other times, that Body of Christ groans from the cross, weighed down by blood, hurt, scars, sin — near dead. It's the same with us. Sometimes we are so hopeful, and other times we become burdened by sin and pain. And yet, like the Church itself, we find our balance in the person of Jesus, who is Himself, in the words of St. Augustine, ever ancient and yet ever new.

⤫

St. Philip Neri compiled a list of seven Roman churches where pilgrims could obtain indulgences. Today the Seven Pilgrim Churches of Rome are St. Peter's, St. John Lateran, St. Paul Outside-the-Walls, St. Maria Maggiore, St. Lawrence Outside-the-Walls, the Holy Cross in Jerusalem, and the Sanctuary of Our Lady of Divine Love. The last one was added by Pope John Paul II during the Jubilee Year 2000, but many pilgrims still prefer to visit the original seventh church — St. Sebastian at the Catacombs.

Oxygen Mask

It seems like I spend half my life on airplanes. I can lip synch the pre-takeoff safety announcement. But one thing has been bugging me for years. Why do the instructions say to attach your own oxygen mask before helping others with theirs? That seems backward, doesn't it? Shouldn't we first help our babies, kids, or weak, elderly, sick companions? Shouldn't our first duty be to save them?

So I finally asked the flight attendant.

She smiled. "It seems logical, I admit, that you would want first to take care of the kids and the weak. But it makes more sense that you first make sure you have enough oxygen, precisely so that you can then care for and protect the ones entrusted to you. If you black out, both you and the one depending on you are in big trouble."

Now it makes sense: if I don't have air to breathe, I can't help those counting upon me for their air. That reminds me of the maxim of classic Catholic spirituality, *"Nemo dat quod non habet"* — "nobody can give what he/she does not have." Or, as St. Bernard observed, "Be a reservoir before you are a channel."

Before we can begin to help others, we need to breathe oxygen for the soul, the breath of the Holy Spirit, sanctifying grace. We need to drink life-giving water from the most sublime, deepest well of all, the Heart of Christ. We need to fill our own beings with the love of God.

After all, if we don't have it in ourselves, we can't give it to others who need it.

❧

St. Bernard of Clairvaux, a twelfth-century French abbot, is one of the Doctors of the Church. Many of his pithy sayings are well known, even if people don't know that he was the author.

- *"Hell is full of good wishes or desires."*
- *"You will find something far greater in the woods than you will find in books. Stones and trees will teach you that which you will never learn from masters. He who prays and labors lifts his heart to God with his hands."*
- *"Prayer is a wine that makes glad the heart of humankind."*

According to the Order of Melchizedek

I love the priesthood. I am head over heels in love with Jesus and His bride — and mine — the Church. Nothing gives me more joy than celebrating Mass, preaching, hearing confessions, baptizing, witnessing marriages, anointing the sick, and being with God's people, whose prayers and encouragement keep me going. Yep, I've had heartburn and headaches, but I'd do it all over again. So would 92 percent of my brother priests, the pollsters tell us.

I love my brother priests. They have stuck with it through some of the toughest years of change in the history of the Church. Those my age and older have seen the priesthood go from a position of influence and prestige to one of derision and decline. They've watched their best friends leave active ministry. The hard right attacks them for being modernists; the way out left dismisses them as oppressive patriarchs. They are branded as abusers of youth, even though the percentage of priests who have tragically done so is less than among teachers, coaches, physicians, counselors, child-care workers, baby-sitters, and even parents.

They watch their numbers shrink; so, they take a second parish, give up the only assistant pastor they had in a behemoth parish, or postpone retirement a few years. Liturgical and catechetical vigilantes from both wings are ready to nail them after each Mass or homily. Rosie O'Donnell regularly terms them sexually repressed because of their celibacy. They are fodder for the late-night comedians

Yet, our priests keep at it. They smile, they pray, they trust, they persevere. They know from their theology that the vitality of the Church and the efficacy of the sacraments do not depend on their virtue, and they're sure glad about that. But most of them work as if it did all depend on them, while praying hard because they acknowledge that it really all depends on the Lord.

When all is said and done, our priests do it because they are in love, hopelessly in love, with a Lord whom they cannot see but who is as real as can be, and hopelessly in love with a Church, who at times is a knockout of a bride, but at other times might seem cold and distant.

I love this priesthood.

I love these priests.

I hope you do, too.

◈

Most gracious Heavenly Father,

We thank you for our faithful priests and bishops, whose spiritual fatherhood and example of fidelity, self sacrifice, and devotion is so vital to the faith of your people.

May our spiritual fathers be guided by the examples of Sts. Peter and Paul, all the Apostles, and their saintly successors. Give them valiant faith in the face of confusion and conflict, hope in time of trouble and sorrow, and steadfast love for you, for their families, and for all your people throughout the world. May the light of your Truth shine through their lives and their good works.

Assist all spiritual fathers, that through your grace they may steadily grow in holiness and in knowledge and understanding of your Truth. May they generously impart this knowledge to those who rely on them.

Through Christ our Lord. Amen.[*]

Our Present Future

On one of his first trips abroad, Pope Benedict XVI traveled to Australia to join youth from around the world for prayer, celebration, song, friendship, and witnessing to the faith at World Youth Day in Sydney.

These gatherings, now held every three years in different countries, were the idea of Pope John Paul II. They have now become much-anticipated events, with countless numbers of adults

---

* http://www.wf-f.org/Priests-prayer.html

pointing to one of the past celebrations as dramatic moments of conversion, grace, and mercy in their own journey of faith.

The amazing success of World Youth Day is only one exhibit in a case of surprising hope documented by religious researchers: the enthusiastic faith of youth and young adults in the Church.

At a time of otherwise bad news, studies show us young people are recovering a vibrant sense of Catholic faith, prayer, worship, and pastoral charity. True, a lot of young people still drift away from or reject the Church, but many are joining or renewing their own sense of solidarity with the Church.

Can we find any common characteristics of these dynamic "new faithful," our youth? For one, they love and believe in Jesus personally. They read His Word in the Bible; they savor prayer to and with Him.

Two, they love the Eucharist not only in the Mass, but also in His Real Presence in the Blessed Sacrament.

Three, they want the truth of Church teaching. "Tell us what God has revealed," they ask. "Tell what Christ has told us, what the Church teaches. Do not 'water it down.' Do not give us opinions or dissent. Tell us the hard, demanding truth."

Four, they have a strong sense of the mercy of God. They admit that, as eager as they are to hear the unvarnished truth of the teaching of the Church in faith and morals, at times they cannot personally accept it or live up to it. They know, then, that they need the Lord's grace and mercy through the Sacrament of Penance!

Five, they relish the community of the Church. Enjoying friendship with peers who share their values and beliefs is important to them, especially since the culture in which they live is often at odds with their convictions.

Finally, they want faith in action, and thus participate in projects of service and charity. To love the poor, to respect all human life, to work for justice and peace, is essential for these committed young people.

Our youth are not just the future of the Church we love. They are the present.

❧

World Youth Day was founded by Pope John Paul II in 1986 as a way to bring Catholic youth together. Thousands, most of them under twenty-one, gather every three years to explore the unity of faith amid the numerous cultures of the world. World Youth Days have been held in such diverse locations as Rome, Buenos Aires, Denver, Manila, Toronto, and Sydney.

Appearances Can Be Deceiving

You wouldn't think it was a gathering of particularly religious folks. After all, they were all decked out in leather vests and black boots, proud of their Harley Davidsons, revving up for the Vince Lombardi ride on behalf of a cancer cure.

I was to lead a prayer and give a blessing.

Would I find much faith in their gathering? I wondered.

Then one showed me the little plastic angel he always carried with him for protection.

Another pointed out the teddy bear he had in his saddlebag, the gift of a little child from a family he had stopped to help after their car had wrecked.

One had a rosary on the handlebar.

Another had a small Bible in his tool kit.

A few others talked about sensing God's presence in the beauty of nature as they rode though the countryside, and asked me to pray for friends who were sick or struggling.

Almost all wore a cross.

They all quieted down, bowed their heads, and closed their eyes when I invited them to pray.

Yes, I had found faith. I'll be darned, I concluded, this *was* a gathering of religious folks.

We often rail against the "secularism" of our "evil age." And, Lord knows, there's plenty of evidence around us to back up a tempting despair that the world has "gone to hell in a hand basket."

But God has not, and will not, give up on us, and — as I was reminded in the strangest of places, a gathering of bikers who looked more frightening than faithful — most of us have not given up on God, either.

Maybe instead of groaning that everybody has gone pagan, secular, and faithless on us, we ought to rejoice in the spark of belief, hope, and goodness that we almost unfailingly find in people — even those decked out in chains, tattoos, leather jackets, and black boots.

❧

Did you know there is a patron saint of motorbikers? St. Columbanus, a seventh-century Irish missionary, has that honor. Apparently, he was quite handsome, because all of his biographers comment on his appearance. Among the miracles attributed to him are the multiplication of bread and beer for his fellow monks, destroying a cauldron of beer being prepared for a raucous festival by simply blowing on it, and taming a bear to be used to plough fields. Why he is the patron of bikers isn't clear, however.

Martha and Mary

e know from the gospels that Our Lord very much enjoyed the companionship and hospitality of Martha and Mary from Bethany. Like many sets of sisters, they were very different. Martha was active, hyperkinetic, and very busy. We see her cooking, setting the table, bustling about taking care of their guest. On the other hand, Mary was calm, passive, contemplative, unhurried. She's content to sit at the Master's feet, listen to him, converse with him, and savor his presence.

This upsets Martha. You really can't blame her. She complains to Jesus about her sister, asking him to command Mary to get off her backside and pitch in on the chores. We can almost picture Our Lord smiling as he defends Mary and calms Martha down.

Jesus defends — actually, exalts — the contemplative side. He compliments Mary, who, he observes, "has chosen the better part" (Lk 10:42).

Not that Our Lord criticizes the active dimension. We know from his other teachings that service, ministry, and active apostolates are very important to him. Besides, he's hungry, and we can assume he is looking forward to Martha's meal. It's just that he realizes that his disciples need both an active and a contemplative side.

As Catholics, we are blessed to have contemplative religious orders in our midst. You do not see their schools, hospitals, soup kitchens, or day care centers. As a matter of fact, you don't even see them. They remain secluded, enclosed, silent, constantly praying with us and for us. They imitate Mary.

Their life is hardly soft and cushy. Anybody who tries to "pray for a living" knows that it is demanding work, but we Marthas would be lost without them.

✖

Sometimes the various Marys of the New Testament get a bit confusing. Besides Mary, the Blessed Virgin, six other Marys are mentioned. First is Mary of Bethany, the sister of Martha as well as Lazarus, who was raised from the dead. Then there is Mary Magdalene, from whom Jesus cast out seven devils. And finally, come the mother of Joses, the wife of Clopas, the mother of James, and the mother of Mark — all of whom may be different people. However, the woman who anointed the feet of Jesus with her hair and oil is never named, even though she is sometimes incorrectly associated with Mary Magdalene.

Looking for the "Perfect" Church

I really shouldn't admit it, because it was not a "nice" thing for me to say, but this couple's letter bordered on the snobbish. They wrote to inform me that they were leaving the Church because it had become "too embarrassing, too tawdry" for them. All the scandals, all the corruption! Tsk tsk! It was just too much for their noble souls. They concluded they were going to find "a better, more perfect Church."

"Good luck," I wrote back. "We'll miss you. And, I sure hope you'll come back home. Oh, and, by the way, if you do find 'a better, more perfect Church,' you'd better not join, because then it won't be perfect anymore!"

Maybe not the most charitable thing to say, but it's true.

Other pastors tell me how often they receive these sad letters, so I'm not alone. One day we'll get a note, "We're leaving the Church because it is no longer true to the spirit of Vatican II" (which of course means that the Church is not true to what that person thinks she should be). The next day another card comes, "We're leaving the Church because she's no longer the pure, unchanging Church I remember as a child in the 1950s" (of course, the Church was never "unchanging" or without faults, as even a cursory knowledge of history tells us.)

Does the Church need reform? Yep! She has from the beginning. As the Latin adage goes, *Ecclesia semper reformanda* — "the Church always in need of reform." So, what do we do? Let these people leave, I guess, pray they come back and keep plodding along, as we have for 2000 years, because, when all is said and done, it's not my Church, our Church, at all. It's Christ's Church.

<hr>

"My Lord, turn the eyes of your mercy upon your people, and upon the mystical body of the Holy Church, for you will be the more glorified if you pardon so many creatures.... For what is it to me if... the clouds of darkness cover your spouse, when it is my own sins, and not those of your other creatures, that are the principal cause of this? I desire, then, and beg of you, by your grace, that you have mercy on your people."
— St. Catherine of Siena, "Dialog"

To Serve the Poor

Most of us have heard of the St. Vincent de Paul Society, but did you know that it wasn't founded by St. Vincent? St. Vincent de Paul was a seventeenth century French priest who, in company with Louise de Marillac, brought about renewal in the Church, particularly by better formation of priests, and daily service to the poor. A hundred and fifty years after Vincent lived, a young intellectual in Paris, Frederick Ozanam, was searching for a way to make his own faith, and that of his companions, more meaningful. This small band formed a group whose ideal was to serve the poor on the streets in the spirit of Christ. They took St. Vincent as their patron, and from this came the St. Vincent de Paul Society as we know it.

Men — and now women, too — come together in this society first of all to strive for holiness. The St. Vincent de Paul Society is not a nice hobby, or a group of "do-gooders." They see it as a way of life, as an invitation to follow Christ more closely, and consider prayer, the Eucharist, and the spiritual support of one another to be essential.

In the spirit of St. Vincent de Paul and Blessed Frederick Ozanam, they know, though, that their love of God must bear fruit in love of neighbor, especially the poor. They do this humbly, almost anonymously, so that most of us hardly even know who they are, when they meet, or what they do... unless you're someone in need who approaches the parish for help in paying for medicine, or making the rent, or buying food, or needing a bus pass for a new job, or just out of jail.

The charism of the St. Vincent de Paul Society is to encounter these situations, never as "cases" or "numbers," but as people, with names and stories. The "Vincentians" meet them, hear them out, keep track of them, visit them, animated by the words of Jesus, "as you did it to one of the least of these who are members of my family, you did it to me" (Mt 25:40). Their work is always in confidence, since the family they help may be right down the block, in their own parish, and others need not know their hard times.

If you ask them their charter, their mission statement, they will reply "The Corporal Works of Mercy." Not a bad charter for any of us.

❧

The road to sainthood has four stages. First is "Servant of God." At this point, an official investigation into holiness is opened. Next comes "Venerable," an indication that the person has lived a life of heroic virtue and may be asked for prayer and assistance. The third level is "Blessed," an official statement by the Church that the person is undoubtedly in heaven as evidenced by one miracle attributed to their intercession. Finally comes "Saint," which is made only after proof of a second miracle. Usually, an investigation into sainthood doesn't start until five years after the death of the person, but the pope can waive the waiting period as John Paul II did for Blessed Teresa of Calcutta and Benedict XVI has done for John Paul II.

Communion of Saints

The doctrine of the Communion of Saints tells us that we are intimately united with those who have preceded us in death. We pray with and for them, we can speak with them spiritually, and we long for the day we'll be reunited in heaven.

A couple of days after Dad dropped dead at work at fifty-one years of age, Mom told me her sadness was even deeper because, the night before his death, they had a little spat. She observed to me that it was burdening her that she was never able to say "I'm sorry" to Dad.

"Well, tell him now," I suggested.

"What do you mean?" Mom asked.

"We trust Dad's with the Lord, right?" I inquired.

"I'm hopeful he is," Mom replied.

"Then he can talk to God, and we can talk to God. Ask God to let Dad know you're sorry."

That's the Communion of Saints. Not some séance, but a childlike belief that "the souls of the just are in the hands of God," and that we belong to a supernatural family that is not limited to the here and now. It is eternal.

Which brings me to Purgatory. Not that Purgatory is eternal, but that the people there are in need of our prayers. We, of course, do not believe in the caricature of purgatory as a place where the souls of imperfect people are waiting for us here on earth to "buy" or "earn" their way to heaven, as if eternal salvation were something other than a free gift from God given us through the merits of his Son Jesus. But we do believe that there is a time of final purification for those souls who still need the cleansing of the Lord's mercy before entrance into heaven. When we pray for those we love who are undergoing that cleansing, we help them enter more quickly into the glory of God.

I pray for those who have gone before me, like my dad, and I hope that when my time comes, someone will be praying for me... in the Communion of Saints.

"I would go so far as to say that if there were no purgatory, then we would have to invent it, for who would dare say of himself that he was able to stand directly before God? And yet, we do not want to be, to use an image from Scripture, a 'pot that turned out wrong,' that has to be thrown away; we want to be put right. Purgatory basically means that God can put the pieces back together again, that he can cleanse us in such a way that we are able to be with Him and stand in

the fullness of life… together in one enormous symphony of being."

— POPE BENEDICT XVI
God and the World, 2002

Sinners Wanted

What is the greatest need for the Church today?

Do we need more people at Mass, more priests, more vocations?

Do we need more committed marriages, more solid families, more efforts on behalf of social justice, peace, pro-life, and charity?

Do we need more schools, more lifelong faith formation, more parishes?

Do we need more money and strategic planning?

Do we need more change in the Church's doctrine and practice, or more rigorous enforcement of faith and morals?

What I think the Church needs is more sinners!

I mean it! We lack persons who humbly recognize their own sins and are willing to confess them.

A good friend of mine is pastor of one of the most prestigious parishes anywhere. His parishioners include wealthy movers and shakers, prominent leaders in business, government, education, and healthcare. It's an attractive parish complex with a stunning array of services and ministries, and gads of cash to fund them. If he were crass, he'd say, "I got it made." You can imagine how stunned his people were one Sunday when he told them he was thinking of requesting a transfer.

"You don't need me here," he explained as the people gasped. "Like Jesus, I came to call sinners. And apparently we have none here. I've heard maybe a half-dozen confessions since I got here six months ago. You're obviously all saints; I came to serve sinners. You don't need me."

I don't know if confessions increased, but I hope so, since all of us "have sinned and fall short of the glory of God" (Rom 3:23).

When was the last time you went to Confession?

> O my God,
> I am heartily sorry for
> having offended Thee,
> and I detest all my sins,
> because I dread the loss of heaven,
> and the pains of hell;
> but most of all because
> they offend Thee, my God,
> Who are all good and
> deserving of all my love.
> I firmly resolve,
> with the help of Thy grace,
> to confess my sins,
> to do penance,
> and to amend my life.
> Amen.

CHAPTER FIVE

The Communion of Saints

St. Peter

The star of the Easter season liturgy — after our risen Savior, of course — has to be St. Peter. We see him "in charge" in the gospel episodes and in most of our readings from the Acts of the Apostles. In the latter, he is the proto-preacher, the premier evangelist of the tiny apostolic community.

I find myself asking as I hear these powerful passages, "Is this the same guy that three times denied even knowing Jesus that first Good Friday? The same apostle who could not run away fast enough from his Lord in need? The same man who tried to talk Our Lord out of the cross, who had a bad temper, whose faith was so weak he began to drown in the lake, who was too proud to allow the Master to wash his feet? Is this the same guy who now is boldly preaching, who takes on the religious leaders and Roman authorities, who risks arrest, jail, and scourging for 'the sake of the Name'?"

Yep! Same guy!

What happened? The Resurrection, of course. The power of our Lord's rising from the dead transforms Peter from fear to faith, from cowardice to courage, from pride to prayer. Life was never again the same for Peter, who became the leader, the chief pastor, the first of the apostles, in the nascent Church.

Peter joined the rest of the apostles in their evangelization of the world, going first to Antioch, then, finally, to Rome, where he established the Church, becoming the first bishop there. Ultimately, he was arrested and crucified by Nero's thugs across the Tiber River on the hill called Vaticanus.

The Office of Peter continues in the Church in his successor Pope Benedict XVI.

Think back a few years. The Church — indeed, the world — was mourning the passing of the Pope who will probably be only the fourth in two millennia to earn the title "the Great." Pope John Paul II's funeral was, the commentators agreed, the most phenomenal in world history, attended by millions, watched by most of the world.

"Who could possibly take his place?" we asked.

And then we saw him take his place on the balcony and heard the words:

> I announce to you a great joy:
> We have a Pope!
> Who takes to himself the name of Benedict XVI.

We welcome Peter among us, and, as the classic, ancient dictum has it, *"Ubi Petrus, ibi ecclesia"* — "Where Peter is, the Church is!

ᔕ᙮ᕲ

The name "Benedict" was first taken by a pope in 575. Almost nothing is known about him except that he was Roman and his father's name was Boniface. The second Benedict, who was proclaimed a saint, was elected in 683 and was renowned for his singing voice. After him come numerous other Benedicts, most of whom ruled in Medieval times and at least one of whom was an anti-Pope. Benedict XV was elected at the start of World War I and made valiant attempts to broker peace.

St. Paul

The case has been made that, after Jesus Himself, no figure has had a more profound impact on Christianity than St. Paul. Hardly a Sunday goes by that we do not hear from St. Paul in the Liturgy of the Word. His faith has shaped ours.

What's interesting is that unlike Peter, Paul did not know Jesus while He was with us physically here on earth.

It did not take much faith for Peter to acknowledge Jesus as the Son of God. Peter was with our Lord daily for the three years of the Master's public life. Peter heard Him teach, saw His miracles, shared his friendship. Heck, even an avowed atheist would profess Jesus as divine if he, like Peter, saw him raise the dead, feed thousands, walk on water, cure lepers, undergo transfiguration, and come back from the dead!

Paul had no such luxury. He only knew Jesus by faith. True, Paul had a genuine, personal encounter with Christ while on the road to Damascus, which humbled him and changed his name and his life forever. But Paul never walked with Jesus, never ate with Him, never saw Him suffer and die. He accepted Jesus as his Lord and Savior by faith.

This gives Paul immense credibility, because he's just like us. None of us was with Jesus during His three years of public life, yet we are expected to put our life on the line for this Christ, to believe He is the Son of God, Our Lord and Savior, the Way, the Truth, and the Life, without ever seeing Him, touching Him, hearing Him in his bodily form. Paul's faith, hope, and love in and for Jesus are passionate, personal, transforming, life-changing, life-giving, now and in eternity.

Truly, he is our ally, our patron, our apostle.

In the summer of 2009, a scientific investigation into a tomb at the Basilica of St. Paul Outside-the-Walls in Rome confirmed what pilgrims have believed for 2000 years — it is the final resting place of St. Paul's mortal remains. Carbon dating of bone fragments indicated that they belonged to someone

who had lived in the first or second century. Tradition has
always claimed that Paul was beheaded and buried there in
A.D. 67.

Blessed Teresa of Calcutta

Throughout my happy years as a priest, I have often had the privilege of celebrating Mass for different communities of the Missionaries of Charity, the order of sisters founded by Blessed Mother Teresa of Calcutta.

Wherever I have been with them for the Eucharist — in St. Louis, in Washington, D.C., or in Rome — I find the chapel in their homes for the poorest of the poor the same: simple, stark, with a crucifix on the front wall, and, underneath, always the same quote from Jesus: "I thirst" (Jn 19:28, NAB), one of the last words of the Master from the cross.

All these years I presumed that Mother Teresa required those two words to be written behind the altar to remind her sisters that they were called to serve the thirsty — and hungry, bleeding, abandoned, dying.

But now it comes out, a decade after her death, that there's perhaps another cogent reason behind her choice of those two words.

Her writings have revealed that Mother Teresa herself was often spiritually thirsty, her own beautiful soul frequently dry and parched as she herself sensed a profound abandonment, dejection, and frustration of her spirit. This great woman, of towering faith, hope, and charity, herself often looked at her Lord and whispered, "I thirst."

Mother Teresa's own bouts of spiritual darkness are the central theme of a new book, *Come, Be My Light*, by Fr. Brian Kolodiejchuk, himself a Missionary of Charity, and the postulator (promoter) of Mother's cause for hopefully eventual canonization as a saint.

His work included a rigorous review of all her writings and letters, and therein he found that this great woman experienced hours, days, weeks, months, long years when her prayer seemed sterile, her faith limp, her hope dim, her love of God tepid. She wrote, with moving humility and honesty, how she often at times even wondered if God had in fact abandoned her.

For thirty-five years, Mother Teresa has been a beacon for me. She animated vibrant belief, an unquenchable hope, an unflagging love, an indomitable joy. She was an inspiration. Now that I know about her own interior struggle, I am inspired by her all the more. I love her and trust her more than ever. No "plaster saint," she. She's as real, as genuine, as flesh and blood as Jesus Himself. For those of us who often sense spiritual fatigue, frustration, and fear — count me in — she's more a model than ever.

In her own spiritual sufferings, which she never hid but humbly shared, and which Pope John Paul II spoke about in his homily at the Mass of her beatification, she was more united with Jesus than ever. With Him, on the cross, she prayed, "I thirst," and uttered with Him, "My God, my God, why have you forsaken me?" (Mt 27:46).

As Fr. Brian observes, "Mother was not only sharing in the physical poverty of her poor, but also the sufferings of Jesus. His longing for union and meaning as expressed in Gethsemane and on the cross."

Through her "dark night of the soul" — to borrow a poetic phrase of another spiritual giant, St. John of the Cross, who also went through spiritual agony — she kept at it, she trusted, she never gave up, she persevered.

No wonder. She's the one who noted, "God does not expect us to be successful. He only asks us to be faithful." Blessed Mother Teresa of Calcutta, pray for us!

◈

"Jesus died on the cross because that is what it took for him to do good to us — to save us from our selfishness in sin. He gave up everything to do the Father's will — to show us that we too must be willing to give up everything to do God's will — to love one another as He loves each of us. If we are not willing to give whatever it takes to do good to one another, sin is still in us. That is why we too must give to each other until it hurts."

— BLESSED TERESA OF CALCUTTA,
NATIONAL PRAYER BREAKFAST,
WASHINGTON, D.C., FEB. 3, 1994

St. Joseph

It was a cold, blustery, icy winter day. I had morning Mass and then a visit at one of our Catholic schools. Before I vested for the Eucharist, I ducked into the boys' bathroom, only to find the janitor scrubbing the floor. The smell of antiseptic almost knocked me over.

"Oh, come on in, Archbishop. It won't bother me. It's just that I want to keep these bathrooms as clean as I can. With all this flu and stuff going around, I want our kids to be as safe from germs as possible!"

"God bless you!" I replied, as I thanked God for a man who saw his work, about as basic and as down to earth as you can get, as a chance to help and protect God's children!

That janitor viewed his labor as God wants all of us to: as an invitation to cooperate with God's infinite care for His creation. The Lord was protecting His children and tending to their well-being and health through the toil of this humble janitor. This worker was truly an agent of God's labor of caring for His creation and His creatures!

May 1 is the feast of St. Joseph the Worker. The principal feast of St. Joseph, foster father of Jesus and spouse of the Virgin Mary, is March 19. But Pope Pius XII instituted this second celebration, which honors Joseph as a laborer, in 1955.

Pope Pius was shrewd. May 1 was the big Communist holiday. The Marxists wanted the workers of the world to unite in revolution and usher in an atheistic, totalitarian dictatorship of the proletariat. By establishing their festival day as St. Joseph's feast day, Pius XII stole their thunder.

The Communists, though, did have a point. Cutthroat capitalism had treated the worker as a cog in a machine, and taken much of the pride, value, and dignity out of work.

This feast spoke volumes: the only begotten Son of God had an earthly father who was a carpenter, and grew up in a home where labor enriched, nourished, and was looked upon as noble and virtuous.

Work, as Pope John Paul II would later teach, was an opportunity to cooperate with the Creator in His ongoing care for His creation and His creatures. Our toil, no matter how tedious, is thus filled with meaning and purpose. Jesus learned that watching His earthly father, St. Joseph, saw, hammer, and build. I absorbed that seeing my own dad labor day-in and day-out so he could nourish, sustain, and care for his family.

And I saw it again as that janitor mopped the toilet floors to keep those kids healthy.

❧

Often we envision St. Joseph as an old man with balding pate and stooped gait, standing protectively beside his teenage wife, Mary. That may be true. But it may not. All we know for sure about Joseph's history is that he was from Bethlehem, that he lived in Nazareth, and that he worked as a carpenter. The idea of his being an aged widower is probably derived from the apocryphal "History of Joseph the Carpenter" which dates to the fifth century. Modern representations in art often show him as a much younger man, actively working and caring for his family.

St. Martha

Maybe it's because I enjoy a hearty meal.

Perhaps it's because I have so often been the recipient of gracious hospitality.

Or, it could just be that my dear grandma — "Nonnie Martie" — had her name.

Whatever the reason, I have always loved St. Martha.

We know her well from the gospels. She, her sister Mary, and her brother Lazarus were among Our Lord's most cherished friends. He often enjoyed their hospitality at their home in Bethany, located just a couple miles walk outside of Jerusalem.

What can we learn from her?

For one, the beauty of hospitality.

St. Benedict observed, *"Venit hospes, venit Christus"* — "When a guest comes, Christ comes."

That was literally true for St. Martha. To heartily welcome guests, to make them feel at home, to see that they enjoy a good meal and can rest and relax... yes, hospitality is a real virtue, and St. Martha exemplifies it.

Two, we can learn the joy of friendship from her. Jesus Christ is true God, but he is also true man. He very much savored the human blessing of rich companionship with others. We know how close He was to Martha. It was she who welcomed Jesus and cooked for Him. And it is to her that Jesus said, "I am the resurrection and the life" (Jn 11:25).

Three, St. Martha helps us appreciate those behind the scenes. Martha was the one cooking in the kitchen, while her sister and brother chatted with the Lord. She knew there was work to be done if they were going to welcome their guest properly, enjoy His friendship, and put out a decent meal.

At any big parish event, my first pastor would always say to me, "Make sure you go back to the kitchen and thank all the workers, and stick around when the party's over to thank the clean-up workers. They're behind the scenes and don't get any credit." They're the St. Marthas. There's a lot of them in life, and there's a lot of them in the Church, thank God.

Hospitality. Friendship. The great example of those behind the scenes.

Good lessons from St. Martha.

Legend has it that after the Resurrection St. Martha traveled to what is now France with her brother and sister. While her brother, Lazarus, allegedly became a bishop/martyr and her sister, Mary, a recluse hermit, Martha is said to have founded a convent at Aix-en-Provence. Called in French la travailleuse de Dieu, *the worker for God, she is the patron of cookery and of housewives.*

Patron Saints

*W*hen I was in second grade, Sister Mary Bosco, our teacher, spoke to us about our patron saints, and how important they are. She then asked each of us who our patron saint was. I, of course, responded, "St. Timothy." Sister, replied, "But, which one? There are quite a few of them."

I figured I better go right to the source. So, I asked mom that afternoon after school, "Mom, which St. Timothy am I named after?"

Mom replied, "You're named after your grandpa. And, believe me, he was no saint!"

Not much help there!

Anyway, I take Timothy, the disciple of St. Paul, the first bishop of Ephesus, as my patron saint.

To have a patron saint is a powerful and beautiful part of our Catholic Faith. We as individuals have them — claimed at Baptism and Confirmation — and parishes have them, dioceses have them, hospitals have them, clubs and organizations have them, causes and professions claim them, nations and countries appeal to them.

Why?

Well, because we belong to a family that extends beyond the here and now. We are members of a supernatural family called the Communion of Saints. Our Blessed Mother, the angels, the apostles, the martyrs, women and men of heroic virtue of every time and place are all part of our spiritual family. When we claim one of these to be a patron, he or she becomes a model for us, and a helper in heaven.

In Italy, where I lived for several years, they take patron saints very seriously. Everybody has a patron saint. Their *onomastico* — the feast day of their patron saint — is as important as their birthday. *The Messagero*, the major daily newspaper in Rome, lists the feast day of the saint on the Masthead every day. The Vatican even has a holiday on the feast of the baptismal patron saint of the current Pope. (Romans are upset because the feast day of Pope Benedict's baptismal patron — St. Joseph — was already a holiday!).

Many of us here in the United States mourn the weakening of the tradition of patron saints. A recent study tells us that names for newborns tend to come from soap operas, TV shows, and movies. So, here's an invitation: parents, give your baby a saint's name, either as a first or as a middle name. There are thousands of them. If, for whatever reason, you do not choose a precise saint's name, still entrust your baby to a particular saint, and tell your child who it is when he or she gets older.

A second invitation, this one to our young people preparing for reception of the Sacrament of Confirmation: choose a name of a saint for your confirmation name. If your baptismal first or middle name is that of a saint, you can keep that one, if you wish, but everybody is free to choose a new saint's name for confirmation.

Let's begin to reclaim this wonderful tradition of patron saints!

❧

St. Timothy of the New Testament was the son of a Greek father and a Jewish convert mother. A friend and travel companion of St. Paul, he accompanied Paul on his second missionary journey. Tradition tells us that after Paul's death Timothy went to Ephesus where he became a bishop. He was stoned to death when he protested a celebration in honor of the goddess Diana.

CHAPTER SIX

Our Mother

Our Lady, Undoer of Knots

I'm always fascinated by the different titles Mary has in the Church. The abundant names we give her serve as testimony to the influence she has in our life. These designations can describe an event — the Annunciation, the Assumption, Sorrowful Mother — or can almost be at times a "job description" of her duties in the Church — Refuge of Sinners, Health of the Sick, Comforter of the Afflicted, Gate of Heaven, Perpetual Help, or Star of the Sea. Then there are titles that come from her apparitions — Guadalupe, Lourdes, Fatima, or Knock come to mind. And different countries honor her under various banners, such as Our Lady of Czestochowa or Our Lady of Pompeii.

Just when I thought I had heard them all, I learned a new one: Mary, Undoer of Knots! The friend who introduced me to this one travels the world helping people undo the knots in women and men tied up emotionally after the horror of an abortion and testifies to Mary's efficiency under this intriguing title.

Listen to how one booklet describes her:

> With the infinite love of a Mother and moved by her extraordinary power of intercession with her son Jesus, Mary, the One who Unfastens the Knots of our life, comes to you today and she comes beautiful, triumphant, splendid and gracious to meet you, bringing with her the heavenly court to unfasten the knots of your life.
>
> How great is her love and the love of her Son for you. He wants you to discover this love because it will dry the tears from your eyes and move the gracious hands of Mary to undo all the knots which afflict you so.
>
> Through her we reach Salvation; through her the knots in our life can be undone. And who does not have them?

But what knots are these? Those problems that we have for years and years and for which we do not see any solution.

Knots of discord in your family, lack of understanding between parents and children, disrespect, violence; the knots of deep hurts between husband and wife, the absence of peace and joy in the home. Knots of anguish and despair of separated couples, the dissolution of the family; knots of the suffering of a drug addict son, sick or separated from the home or God; knots of alcoholism, our vices and those of our loved one. Knots of hurts and resentment that so torture our heart; guilt feelings, the practice of abortion, the sickness that does not get better, depression, unemployment, fear, solitude.... Knots of lack of trust, pride, a sinful life.*

Ah, the knots of our life! How they suffocate our soul, beat us down, betray our heart's joy and even bind our will to continue living. Knots separate us from God, chaining our very being and strangling our faith, keeping us from flinging like children into the arms of God, our loving Father.

The Virgin Mary does not want these knots to continue anymore in your life. She comes to you today asking you to give her these snarls to undo them one by one.

Today, recognize the greatness of your Mother, Undoer of Knots, and let her lead you to know the wonders that will be done

---

* Quoted from Dr. Suzel Frem Bougerie, author of *Mary, Undoer of Knots Novena*. Reprinted with permission of the author and of The National Sanctuary of Mary Undoer of Knots. The Novena is also available in English and can be acquired at: Mary Undoer of Knots, 271 Richvale Drive South, Unit # 1, Brampton, ON, L6Z 4W6 Canada; (905) 495-4614; novena@maryundoerofknots.com; www.maryundoerofknots.com. The National Sanctuary of Mary Undoer of Knots receives pilgrims from around the world: Santuário Maria Desatadora dos Nós; Rua Alexandre de Gusmão, 80 Jd. Guanabara, 13080-100 Campinas, SP, Brazil; www.mariadesatadoradosnos.com.br.

for you. Come close to her now. See her beauty. Entrust your afflictions to her, knowing that she will unravel all the knots of your life.

∾⤬∾

The basis for calling Mary "Our Lady, Undoer of Knots" probably dates back to Irenaeus who wrote in the second century "the knot of Eve's disobedience was untied by Mary's obedience; for what Eve bound by her unbelief, Mary loosed by her faith." A painting, showing Mary untying a white ribbon, has recently become popular and probably is of Baroque origin.

What Would Your Mother Think?

I could not get out of my head the story I heard from a good friend who is a missionary in Kenya. It seems that a seventy-three-year-old Daughter of Charity, also a missionary, walked into a burglary in process at a religious house in Nairobi. The thieves were rough, ruthless, vicious, driven by violence and probably drugs. After they had pillaged the house, one of the criminals turned to Sister and leered at her, "Pull up your dress." His intention was clear: he was going to rape this seventy-three-year-old nun.

With all the calmness she could muster, she looked at him and replied, "What would your mother think of you?"

Can you imagine? To a raging, pillaging rapist, she says words you would use to chide a six-year-old after he had said a nasty word: "What would your mother think of you?"

How did the potential rapist react? He stopped, looked at Sister, thought a moment, and left her alone.

Those simple words had worked.

That appeal to his mother had been effective.

"What would your mother think of you?"

It seems that, no matter how low we may sink in life, how many mistakes, sins, or crimes we may have committed, the thought of our mother brings back all that is right, good, decent, noble, and honorable. Mothers represent the way things should be, not how bad they are. Mothers remind us that we are destined for greatness, for virtue.

Bring on Mary, the Mother of Jesus, the Mother of God, the Mother of us all. In her very person she reminds us of the dignity that God the Father intended for all of us: free from sin, close to Him, united to Jesus, taken body and soul to heaven.

So the next time you are feeling tempted to do something you know you shouldn't, ask yourself "What would my mother think?" and act accordingly.

⁂

We usually refer to Mary as the "Mother of God," but members of the Eastern Orthodox Church more commonly refer to her as the Theotokos — *"God-bearer." The Third Ecumenical Council gave Mary that designation, helping to emphasize that her son Jesus was fully God as well as fully man. One of the earliest references to Mary as the "God-bearer" comes from Irenaeus: "The Virgin Mary, being obedient to his word, received from an angel the glad tidings that she would bear God"* (Against Heresies, *5:19:1).*

Homecoming

For me, to go home — to my mom's house — is unfailingly a joy. There, I'm in comfortable and familiar surroundings, with a woman who knows me better than anybody else. With Mom there's no need to impress. Why even bother to impress the woman who changed my diapers? The place is familiar, the conversation natural, the food tastes better, even my old ball glove is there. I always leave refreshed and renewed, wondering why I do not do it more often, and anxious about the sure-to-come day when Mom will not be at home any more — at least in her earthly one.

To go to Mom's house is a blessing indeed, a gift, a renewal. I am reminded of who I am, where I came from, and where I've gone — right and wrong — since leaving there.

That's why I also try to go to one of my spiritual mother's houses, too... Lourdes.

What visiting my mom back in Missouri does for me naturally, being with my blessed Mother, Mary, in this small mountain village in southwestern France, where she once appeared, does for me supernaturally.

I go to Lourdes because I owe her a visit. She has never let me down, and I am in deep debt to her. She has gotten me out of jams, helped a lot of people I love and referred to her, and at times gotten me back on the right path. The conversation is great there, as I spend a lot of time talking with her and her son, who is my best friend — as well as my Lord and my God.

She loves me unconditionally. She listens while I pour out my guts. She is not bored when I tell her what I'm worried about. She promises me she'll help.

She washes me clean in cold spring water, as I will bathe in the miraculous waters and become once again like a baby at the baptismal font.

She'll catch me crying and ask what's wrong. She'll listen as I tell her ways I've hurt her Son and her other children. She'll encourage me to tell her Son "I'm sorry" in the Sacrament of Penance, and I'll stand in line with hundreds of others to do so.

She'll have a family reunion while I'm there at her house, as thousands will come, and I'll see the family in all its "Catholic" diversity again, especially the sick and the searching.

We'll all get together and sing to her every evening as we carry candles and belt out her rosary in half-a-dozen languages.

I go to Lourdes because I need to tell my blessed mother that I love her, I need her, I thank her, and that I always feel at home with her.

❧

The earliest known apparition of Mary is said to have occurred in A.D. 39 when she is alleged to have appeared to St. James the Great in Zaragoza, Spain. This appearance is referred to as Our Lady of the Pillar. Some of the apparitions that have been officially approved by the Church include: Our Lady of Guadalupe, Our Lady of Laus, Our Lady of the Miraculous Medal, Our Lady of La Salette, Our Lady of Pontmain, Our Lady of Fatima, Our Lady of Beauraing, Our Lady of Banneux, Our Lady of Akita, and Our Lady of Lourdes.

Our Lady of Guadalupe

She's pregnant, you know.

She's wearing maternity clothes.

You can tell by the cord around her waist. That was the sign among the Aztecs that a woman was expecting.

That's one of the many reasons I am moved by this sacred depiction of Our Lady — because, for some reason, we do not imagine her as pregnant.

But we should.

For nine months, from the Annunciation (which we celebrate on March 25th) till Christmas, she was pregnant with the Incarnate Word, the son of God, the Savior of the World.

So I often find myself in awe before the image of Our Lady of Guadalupe.

A pregnant mother.

She was aware, as any expectant woman is, that she had to be patient, because there's no rushing the baby. No wonder centuries of longing, waiting, struggling, burdened people have looked to her, and the baby in her womb, with hope.

Remember how she consoled Juan Diego, the man to whom she appeared? Hear her words:

> Listen! Put it into your heart, my dearest son, that the thing that disturbs you, the thing that afflicts you, is really nothing.
>
> Do not let your heart be disturbed.
>
> Am I not here, I who am your Mother?
>
> Are you not under my shadow and my protection?
>
> Am I not the Source of your joy?
>
> Are you not in the hollow of my mantle, in the crossing of my arms?
>
> Do you need anything more?
>
> Let nothing else worry or disturb you.

When I was a seminarian in Rome, I would often take busses in the city. They were unfailingly jammed. One could hardly move. You could never get a seat.

I would always notice a sign on the bus: "Please leave the seats free for the elderly, those wounded in war, and pregnant women."

Our lives are jam-packed. We hardly have room for another thing, but we must leave a seat free for the pregnant woman, the one who carries within her the Son of God, the one who is our Mother, too.

᠆ᢙᢏᢙ᠆

Juan Diego, the man to whom Mary appeared in Mexico, was of Aztec descent. So why is she referred to by a Spanish name? The best explanation is that she spoke to him in his native language, Nahuatl, and called herself "Coatlaxopeuh" which sounds very much like "Guadalupe." When the Spanish priests heard it, they probably assumed it was their own place name. Incidentally, the principal god of the Aztecs was a serpent and Coatlaxopeuh means "the one who crushes the serpent."

The Feasts of Mary

When I was a kid and went almost weekly to the movies, I used to enjoy the "coming attractions." I still do when I get to the rare movie. It gives me something to look forward to.

In a way, Mary, the Mother of the Lord Jesus, and our own spiritual mother, is a "preview," a "coming attraction." She is there to remind us how God first wanted creation to be and how he wants it all to work out.

It's important to remember that Our Lady is not a goddess. She is a human being like you and me. In her, God elevates all humanity and reminds us how he designed creation.

From the start, Our Father intended all of us to be immaculately conceived. He wanted all of us to be free from sin, in perfect union with him, utterly happy in obedience to his will. The first Adam and Eve ruined that dream; the second Adam and Eve, Jesus and Mary, restored it. Mary is hardly less human because she is free from sin. She is more genuinely human, for sin only detracts from humanity's nobility.

Then, through the dogma of her Assumption, God our Father teases us with what he has prepared for us: to be with him, body and soul, for all eternity, in heaven. He wants all of us to be with him forever, just as Mary is now.

The point is that in God's original design, Mary would not have stood out at all. She would have been ordinary. So she's always with us, to remind us how God wants his creation to work out.

Yes, Satan crossed God's original plan by successfully tempting the first Adam and Eve to original sin. But, in an even bigger yes, God crossed Satan's nightmare on Calvary, where the second Adam restored us to His Father's dominion, as the second Eve crushed the serpent's head.

No wonder she is so important to our faith; for she is, in the words of the poet, "Our tainted nature's solitary boast."

The Virgin
By William Wordsworth

> *Mother! whose virgin bosom was uncrost*
> *With the least shade of thought to sin allied;*
> *Woman! above all women glorified,*
> *Our tainted nature's solitary boast;*
> *Purer than foam on central ocean tost;*
> *Brighter than eastern skies at daybreak strewn*
> *With fancied roses, than the unblemished moon*
> *Before her wane begins on heaven's blue coast;*
> *Thy Image falls to earth. Yet some, I ween,*
> *Not unforgiven the suppliant knee might bend,*
> *As to a visible Power, in which did blend*
> *All that was mixed and reconciled in Thee*
> *Of mother's love with maiden purity,*
> *Of high with low, celestial with terrene!*

CHAPTER SEVEN

Workers in the Vineyard

Sanctuary

$\mathcal{S}$anctuary... a holy place, where all God's children are welcome and respected.

Sanctuary... safety, security, inviolability, a harbor, a refuge, a shelter.

Sanctuary... the very word soothes, protects, embraces, welcomes.

So, the poor hounded by the soldiers of the king could claim sanctuary in a church, to remain untouched until they received a fair hearing....

So, runaway slaves could seek sanctuary in churches where they would be safe until it was safe to leave and pursue their yearning for freedom....

So, conscientious objectors to war could find sanctuary where the draft board could not get to them....

Even today immigrants and refugees come for sanctuary rather than be sent back to persecution or torn from their families.

However, of all of the sanctuaries, the most powerful, beautiful, and natural of them all is the mother's womb. There a baby, from the moment of conception, finds security, safety, protection, care. There no threatening power can invade.

At least not until January 22, 1973, and *Roe v. Wade*.

Now, what should be the sanctuary of the womb is the most dangerous of all places for a preborn baby to be.

Now, with abortion on demand, more babies die in the womb than from bombs in Iraq (as terrifying as those are), famine in Darfur (as tragic as that is), or inadequate medical care (as unjust as that is).

This holy sanctuary is now invaded by chemicals, solutions, scissors, knives, scalpels, forceps.

Does this depress you? Understandable.

Does this sadden you? Join the crowd.

Does this shock you? It should.

Does this move you to action? Even better.

Join today's sanctuary movement! Restore nature's safe, secure, unthreatened refuge!

Protect the most innocent, jeopardized person of all — the baby in the womb.

∽✕∾

Roe v. Wade is known to all of us as the Supreme Court case that legalized abortion. What many people don't know is that Jane Roe is the fictitious name given to Norma McCorvey by her attorneys when they decided to bring an abortion case before the Texas courts. In the intervening years, McCorvey has publicly stated her regrets at being involved in the legalization of abortion and has become a Catholic. Incidentally, she never did abort the child she was carrying at the time. Her daughter was given up for adoption.

The Whisper of the Spirit

While in Rome, I came upon a mural depicting a familiar scene in the life of Pope St. Gregory the Great (590–604). It seems the legendary Pope was walking one day through the Roman Forum, where he witnessed children being sold into slavery. He asked where they were from and was told that they were "angles," (the Roman word for the English people). The mural shows a dove, the symbol of the Holy Spirit, fluttering around Pope Gregory's ear, inspiring him to roar out, "They are not 'angles,' they are 'angels.'" This statement not only put an obstacle to the vicious slave trade, but also inspired Pope Gregory to send a missionary to England, the famous St. Augustine of Canterbury.

It is clear that the Holy Spirit is again whispering, if not shouting, into the ear of the people of the Church: the baby in the womb, incipient life in the laboratory, the dying in our nursing homes — these are all angels.

They reflect God's image.

They have life.

They deserve respect.

Those of us who profess a consistent ethic of life believe that human life everywhere is sacred: the embryonic cell; the baby in the womb from conception; the baby born into poverty; those afflicted by war, famine, or persecution; the prisoner on death row; the dying in our hospices and homes; those with handicaps and severe sickness. If we truly believe, we must shout out to a culture of death that is convinced that convenience and utility trump the right to life, "These are angels!"

❧

Only Pope Leo I, Pope Gregory I, and Pope Nicholas I have been given the title "the Great." Pope from 590 to 604, Gregory's influence has come down to us, not only for his zeal in promoting missionary work, especially to the British Isles, but also because of Gregorian chant. While Gregory did not invent this form of plainsong music, tradition has held that he was responsible for assembling it into one of the first antiphonaries.

Pro-Life Homily

I've been close to these two splendid couples for a while. The first couple have five wonderful sons. One of them, the passionate love of his parents and the pride of his brothers, is a special needs child to a very advanced degree. This beautiful boy — with blue eyes that are hypnotic and a smile that melts ice caps — needs constant help to breathe, eat, or even move. He can only communicate with sounds and slight movements, which are always masterfully comprehended by his parents and ever-attentive siblings. He's been close to death countless times, and his mere existence is an eloquent testimony to the resilience of life itself and the power of the love of his family.

This couple became pregnant again, and early tests indicated that the new baby had Down Syndrome. To end the life of their preborn baby never crossed the radar of these parents, but Mom and Dad were realistically and prudently worried about their ability, given their constant attention to their other special needs child, to care for their new baby with their limited resources and energy.

After a lot of family discernment and prayer, they arrived at the tough but eminently understandable and heroic decision that they could best love their new baby by sharing her with a couple eager to adopt a special needs child.

Enter couple number two. I'd only known them a few years, but I'd been praying with and for them for a new baby. They had no children, and it was looking less and less likely that they would. When I telephoned them to inquire as to how they were doing, they told me of their decision to look into adopting a special needs baby and asked if I could help.

Coincidence? You know what Pope John Paul II observed: "Coincidence is what an unbeliever calls providence."

I put these two deeply Catholic couples in touch and then had the joy and honor of baptizing their magnificent new baby in a church jammed with the inspirational blood parents and their wonderful sons and the extended families of the new adoptive mom and dad.

There was not enough tissue to go around as tears of joy were flowing in abundance.

It was bittersweet for the biological parents to give their daughter away, but all they had to do was observe the radiant, tender love of the beaming adoptive mom and dad to know that they had done the right thing.

What was non-negotiable to all four parents was the tiny, frail, new life of that baby, and her well-being.

It was the Church at her best.

It was humanity at its most noble.

It was the most pro-life homily I have ever seen preached.

∽✺∾

Mary, we pray today for all mothers who are afraid to be mothers. We pray for those who feel threatened and overwhelmed by their pregnancy. Intercede for them, that God may give them the grace to say yes and the courage to go on. May they have the grace to reject the false solution of abortion. May they say with you, "Be it done unto me according to your word." May they experience the help of Christian people, and know the peace that comes from doing God's will. Amen. *

To Care for the Sick

Thirty years ago, Pope John Paul II designated the Feast of Lourdes to be the World Day of the Sick, since millions annually flock there for physical, emotional, and spiritual healing.

The sick were our Lord's favorite people. Jesus is the Divine Physician, who healed the sick, and still does.

---

* http://www.priestsforlife.org/prayers/prayertomary.html

It is no surprise, then, that His Church continues to care for His sick. But just what makes a hospital, or healthcare facility Catholic?

One factor would be the very philosophy of the hospital. Their mission is to continue to care and heal in the name of Jesus. They are not in it for profit or for business. They are in it to serve. They must be careful stewards and wise managers, but, for them, it's not a job, but a vocation, an apostolate.

Two, a Catholic hospital or healthcare facility serves the whole person, body, mind, and soul. A vibrant pastoral care department, and a priest available for Mass, Confession, and the Sacrament of Anointing of the Sick, would be the norm in our Catholic institutions.

Three, the poor would receive a particularly warm embrace. The first words a patient would hear would not be, "What kind of insurance do you have?" but "Welcome! What is your name and how can we help you?" The quality of care provided would not be dependent upon one's ability to pay.

Four, there would be visible signs of Christianity. The name itself would indicate the patronage of Jesus, His Mother, one of the saints, or a virtue (e.g., Mercy). One would find a crucifix in every room, statues and religious images all over, a Bible and prayer book in every room, and, of course, a chapel with the Blessed Sacrament reserved for quiet and prayer.

Five, nothing contrary to Catholic moral teaching would ever occur, especially abortion, euthanasia, and mutilations such as vasectomies or tubal ligations.

Six, employees in our institutions would be treated with justice and respect, and would exude a sense of joy, care, patience, and tender service.

May each of our Catholic hospitals and healthcare facilities be a Lourdes where God's favorites, the sick and poor, find dignity, love, care, faith, hope, and healing, and where the presence of Jesus and His mother is tangible.

∾✕∾

The World Day of the Sick was instituted on May 13, 1992, by Pope John Paul II. At that time, he wrote: "To you, dear sick people all over the world, the main actors of this World Day, may this event bring the announcement of the living and comforting presence of the Lord. Your sufferings, accepted and borne with unshakeable faith, when joined to those of Christ take on extraordinary value for the life of the Church and the good of humanity."[*]

The Need for Patience

*A*t a recent district meeting of priests, we began with this poem, written by Fr. Pierre Teilhard de Chardin:

Above all, trust in the slow work of God.
We are all, quite naturally, impatient in everything
    to reach the end without delay.
We should like to skip the intermediate stages.
We are impatient of being on the way
    to something unknown,
        something new,
Yet it is the law of all progress that is made
    by passing through some stages of instability
        and that it may take a very long time.

---

[*] http://www.catholic.org/international/international_story.php?id=32073&page=2

And so I think it is with you.
Your ideas mature gradually. Let them grow.
Let them shape themselves without undue haste.
Do not try to force them on,
    as though you could be today what time
        — that is to say, grace —
    and circumstances
        acting on your own good will
    will make you tomorrow.
Only God could say what this new Spirit
    gradually forming within you will be.

Give our Lord the benefit of believing
    that his hand is leading you
    and accept the anxiety of feeling yourself
        in suspense and incomplete.
Above all, trust in the slow work of God,
    our loving vine-dresser.

Amen.[*]

Fr. Teilhard is on target: we need patience. Our desire for the better tomorrow cannot keep us from doing the good today. In the end, it's God's grace and mercy, not our efforts, that bring about the Kingdom.

If we're impatient with the Lord's guidance of His Church, just imagine for a moment how weary He can become of us! So we keep at it, stumbling along, sometimes jogging, more often crawling, toward the goal. Our best friends are humility, patience, and joy, as we trust "in the slow work of God."

---

[*] Published at http://www.worship.ca/docs/p_62_ptdc.html; from *Pneuma*, Vol. 6, No. 2, Fall, 1999. *Pneuma* is a journal on spiritual direction and formation in the Evangelical Lutheran Church in Canada.

౷

Pierre Teilhard de Chardin (May 1, 1881 – April 10, 1955) was
a French philosopher/theologian and Jesuit priest who studied
as a paleontologist. He published several scientific papers and
was involved in the discovery of Peking Man. In his spiritual
writings, he attempted to make sense of scientific discoveries,
especially about the origin of man, with his Catholic faith.

Take Up Your Cross

I guess I had better write about the cross.
I'd rather not.

It seems negative, somber, sad, and unappealing to talk about
the cross. You wouldn't do it at a dinner party....

Yet there is no avoiding it. According to the Crucified One, we
must carry our cross if we want to follow Him. He came to die on
the cross.

When you think about it, the cross comes to us in three different ways:

The first is in the adversity and agony that life brings all of us as
part of the human condition. Every human being has struggle, sadness, and suffering. Walk the floors of Children's Hospital, drive the
streets of our central cities, watch the news about Darfur and Iraq,
listen to your neighbor's woes, or look into your own heart, and you
will find affliction. Everybody has it; everybody wonders why.

We followers of Jesus have it, too. We call it the cross. Jesus
never promised to take the cross away from us, but now we carry
our cross with Him. He helps us take up our daily cross. We cooperate with Him in the world's redemption, and we believe that the
cross does not have the last word. These are powerful motives for

us to shoulder our crosses. Second, we can voluntarily add the cross to our lives by acts of penance and self-denial. Jesus encouraged fasting and mortification. So does His Church, and not just during Lent, but every day. I know of no saint who did not voluntarily invite the cross into his or her life through such penitential practices. And we're all called to be saints.

Third, the cross comes into our life as we suffer for our faith. We may not suffer literal martyrdom here in America, but we may have to suffer for our faith in more subtle ways:

Ask the nurse who, after six years, still has no promotion because she will not assist at abortions in the hospital.

Listen to the attorney, reprimanded by the senior partners at the firm, because he's active in promoting affordable housing for the poor, to the discomfort of one of the firm's most cherished clients, a slumlord.

Hear how the researcher is denied a fellowship because he opposes embryonic stem cell destruction.

I could add to the litany of examples, but you get the point: if we take our faith seriously, we will carry a cross, because our world, our culture, opposes us.

The Church is the meeting of the cross bearers, a support group for people with weighty ones. Look around you at Sunday Mass. Everybody has splinters in their shoulders.

❧

Many people think that when the Catholic Church removed the requirement to abstain from eating meat on Fridays, the whole idea of fasting and abstinence was eliminated except during Lent. In fact, the Church never actually stopped meatless Fridays at all. The Church still asks that each Friday be a penitential day during which the faithful join in the suffering of Christ on the Cross. *If a person doesn't abstain from meat (which is still prescribed in Canon 1251), some other act of penance must be substituted.*

White Martyrs

Those who suffer persecution and even death because of their faith are called "red martyrs" because their acts of faith involve the shedding of blood. This is the type of martyrdom we usually recognize, whether the martyrs died during the persecutions in the Roman Empire or in various parts of the world today.

Classically though, the Church recognizes another kind martyrdom — white martyrs. These courageous faithful suffer emotionally, spiritually, or physically for the faith, yet not to the point of shedding blood.

In some ways, if we take our religion seriously, we will all become white martyrs at some time in our lives.

Let me just mention some white martyrs I've recently met who have inspired me profoundly:

The mother who sits night and day at the bedside of her little son as he's hooked up to chemo at Children's Hospital.

The family with four children who have just adopted a special needs baby.

The college student who gets snickered at every Sunday morning in the university dorm as he gets up early to go to Mass.

The young husband who is sticking by his wife for the long haul, even though she's "fallen off the wagon" again in her constant struggle with an addiction to alcohol.

They are all white martyrs. They are suffering because of their faith. No one is after them with torches, machetes, or guns, but their trial is real, their faith enduring, their hope unflagging.

Sooner or later, we'll all be there.

It's part of the dying and rising of Jesus and His people.

⌒⌒⌒

The word "martyr" comes from the Greek word meaning "witness." The first known martyr was St. Stephen who was stoned to death for his belief in Christ. His death is recorded in Acts 6:8–8:3. Even today, an estimated 500 people around the world suffer and die each day for their Faith. One of the most recent martyrs to be canonized is St. Maximilian Kolbe, who died at Auschwitz, on August 14, 1941.

A Grateful Heart

A number of years ago, I called someone to thank her for the amazingly generous gift she had given Catholic Relief Services to help those whose lives had been devastated by the ravages of the 2004 tsunami.

"You're thoughtful to call me," she replied. "But I hardly deserve any thanks. The wealth I have is not mine to hoard. Everything I have — life itself, health, home, family, friends, my country, and, yes, my money, property, and possessions — is God's, not mine. He entrusts it to me to be shared with others. Thank the Lord, not me. I do, everyday."

Is that not a great homily on the concept of Thanksgiving? (By the way, it's also a beautiful definition of stewardship.)

Blessed Mother Teresa observed that the saddest people are those who believe they have no reason to be grateful. She used to remark that she could never fail to be moved by the "thank you" whispered by the dying beggars after she gave them a drink of water.

What makes us great is that we admit we are not.

What makes us rich is to admit that it all really belongs to God.

What increases us is to thank God for what we have.

What fills us up is to acknowledge that we are really quite empty.

What turns us into saints is to confess that we are sinners.

As the poet George Herbert prayed, "O Lord, you have given me so much. Please give me one thing more: a grateful heart."

∞✦∞

George Herbert (April 3, 1593 – March 1, 1633) was both a poet and an Anglican priest. Many of his poems have been set to music, including the famous hymn "Come, My Way, My Truth, My Life." He is also the author of several pithy quotations including "His bark is worse than his bite."

Never Lose the Vision

The line has been haunting me. It came when I was reading Habakkuk 2:3:

> For there is still a vision for the appointed time;
> it speaks of the end and does not lie.
> If it seems to tarry, wait for it;
> it will surely come, it will not delay.

It's said that every community — family, neighborhood, parish, diocese, Church, country, business — needs two essentials to keep it vibrant: memories and dreams.

If all we have are memories, we become a museum. If all we have are dreams, we turn into rootless drifters.

Every day, people remind me of the vision, the dreams:

"We need a new parish out here."

"Please, can the Church open a house for recently paroled prisoners where they can live and get re-integrated into society?"

"We need a new Catholic high school up here."

"We've got to open shelters for women with problem pregnancies."

"Why can't we have Eucharistic Adoration at our parish?"

Someone asked me what's going on in the Church that bothers me. I replied that what really bothers me is what is *not* going on in the Church. All the hopes and needs not being met is what haunts me.

So many needs.

So many requests.

So many demands.

So many great ideas.

I'm not complaining. I'm glad there are so many things that people want. It means we're dreaming. It means it's not all past memories.

It means the vision still awaits its appointed time.

For everything there is a season, and a time for every matter under heaven:

> *a time to be born, and a time to die;*
> *a time to plant, and a time to pluck up what is planted;*
> *a time to kill, and a time to heal;*
> *a time to break down, and a time to build up;*
> *a time to weep, and a time to laugh;*

a time to mourn, and a time to dance;
a time to throw away stones, and a time to gather stones
  together;
a time to embrace, and a time to refrain from
  embracing;
a time to seek, and a time to lose;
a time to keep, and a time to throw away;
a time to tear, and a time to sew;
a time to keep silence, and a time to speak;
a time to love, and a time to hate;
a time for war, and a time for peace.

— ECCLESIASTES 3:1–8

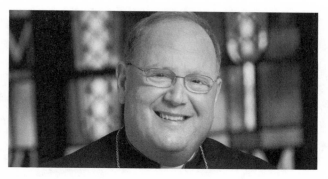

More Insight and Inspiration from Archbishop Dolan...

To Whom Shall We Go?

To Whom Shall We Go? presents the words and actions of St. Peter — along with the direction and insights of Archbishop Timothy Dolan — as a practical, day-to-day example for all of us.

Priests for the Third Millennium

Whether considering a vocation, re-charging a vocation, or simply wanting to better understand a parish priest, Archbishop Dolan sets forth a frank and realistic view of what it takes to be a Catholic priest today.

Called to Be Holy

With encouragement and real-world advice, New York's Archbishop Timothy M. Dolan delivers a radically different approach for becoming a good steward of the Gifts of the Holy Spirit every day.

To order call 800-348-2440 x3

OurSundayVisitor